Best Books
for Boys

Recent Titles in the
Children's and Young Adult Literature Reference Series
Catherine Barr, Series Editor

Best Books for Boys

A RESOURCE FOR EDUCATORS

Matthew D. Zbaracki

Children's and Young Adult Literature Reference
Catherine Barr, Series Editor

LIBRARIES
U N L I M I T E D
A Member of the Greenwood Publishing Group

Westport, Conn. London

Library of Congress Cataloging-in-Publication Data

Zbaracki, Matthew D.
  Best books for boys : a resource for educators / Matthew D. Zbaracki ;
introduction by Jon Scieszka.
      p. cm. — (Children's and young adult literature reference)
  Includes bibliographical references and indexes.
  ISBN 978-1-59158-599-2 (alk. paper)
  1. Boys—Books and reading—United States. 2. Teenage boys—Books and
reading—United States. 3. Children's literature—Bibliography. 4. Young
adult literature—Bibliography. 5. Best books—United States. I. Title.

  Z1039.B67Z23 2008
  028.5'5—dc22   2007051065

British Library Cataloguing in Publication Data is available.

Library of Congress Catalog Card Number: 2007051065
ISBN 978-1-59158-599-2

First published in 2008

Libraries Unlimited, 88 Post Road West, Westport, CT 06881
A Member of the Greenwood Publishing Group, Inc.
www.lu.com

Printed in the United States of America

The paper used in this book complies with the
Permanent Paper Standard issued by the National
Information Standards Organization (Z39.48–1984).

10   9   8   7   6   5   4   3   2   1

For Oliver: My favorite boy

Contents

Foreword

Interested in getting boys reading?

You've come to the right place.

We've been testing kids for thirty years now, and finding that boys are lagging behind girls . . . at every age . . . every year of testing. Now we're finally having the discussion that maybe reading preferences and strategies might be gender-based. Now people are realizing that we can, and should, change how we reach readers. And thank goodness for the teachers and librarians leading this charge for change.

Dr. Matthew Zbaracki is one of those leaders. He has dug into the research, worked with students and teachers in schools, and seen what is going on with kids struggling to read.

The book you are holding in your hands is just what we need — an explanation of what is going on with boys and reading, and a prescription for what we can do to help.

The good news is that there are plenty of things we can do.

The challenge is that we have to make the changes.

So start reading, and let's get boys reading.

Jon Scieszka
Brooklyn, NY, 2007
www.guysread.com

Preface

A number of years ago, while I was working on my dissertation about humorous literature and how it engages readers, I interviewed a few authors about how and why they used humor in their work. Children's book author Jon Scieszka was one of them. He and I kept in touch, and a few years ago we began talking about the issue of boys and reading. Before long Scieszka's book *Guys Write for Guys Read* was published (see page 22) and we began to talk about spreading the word about books and boys. This led to a symposium at the International Reading Association's national convention in Chicago in 2006. That symposium featured an author's panel including Scieszka, Gordon Korman, Will Hobbs, and David Shannon. This presentation led to the idea of creating an anthology of great books for boys. You hold in your hands the result.

The purpose of this book is to provide a resource for school librarians, public librarians, teachers, and parents looking for books that boys will enjoy reading. It's my hope that this resource will help engage young male readers.

The titles I read for inclusion in this book were selected from many sources. I have taught courses in children's literature at the university level for the past six years. During that time I have read many titles that appeal to boys. I have also talked with boys about what they enjoy reading. Colleagues, friends, teachers, librarians, and family have also recommended titles to me. Finally, I consulted professional journals (*The Horn Book*,

The Reading Teacher, and *The Journal of Adolescent and Adult Literature*, for example).

This book will be a valuable resource for professionals who work with male readers. In it they will find outstanding titles in genres including humor, adventure, sports, fantasy, historical fiction, and nonfiction. Just one or two great books can help a boy grow as a reader and even make him a lifelong reader. Use this book, recommend this book, and help to motivate and support the male reader.

Many people helped make this book possible. I thank Jane for all her support during the researching and writing of this book. My family (especially my mother, a former children's librarian) always stopped everything to suggest titles. Dr. Jennifer Geringer also lent support and provided new books to include in this collection. I'd like to thank Ambassador Jon Scieszka for his support from beginning to end. Thanks also go to Gordon Korman, Will Hobbs, and David Shannon for contributing to the cause. Thanks to my colleagues at the University of Northern Colorado, Rhode Island College, and across the country for their support.

Many publishing companies provided me with books. I thank Dina Sherman and Angus Killick for providing me books well before they were published.

I would like to thank Susan C. Olmstead for her excellent copyediting work. Thanks also to Julia Miller and Christine McNaull, who organized the entries and created a great layout for the book. And finally, thank you to Catherine Barr, an outstanding editor, for all your ideas and support.

Chapter 1

Boys and Books

"Boys just don't like to read." Educators have enough proof to suspect that this is more than a myth. We've all seen a boy "reading" while his eyes dart around the room looking at anything — his friends, his teacher, the clock — but the book on his desk while he counts down the minutes until recess.

But research suggests that boys *are* reading — they just may not be reading what teachers and schools deem "acceptable." This in turn tends to turn guys off from reading at all, because they see it as "schoolish" (Smith & Wilhelm, 2002).

Jon Scieszka, named the inaugural National Ambassador for Young People's Literature by the Center for the Book at the Library of Congress (and author of the Time Warp Trio books, *The Math Curse*, *The Stinky Cheese Man and Other Fairly Stupid Tales*, *Squids Will Be Squids*, and many others) is committed to leading boys to reading. He created the Guys Read program (www.guysread.com), a literacy initiative focused on boys. Scieszka also recently compiled a collection of stories written by male authors titled *Guys Write for Guys Read*. In it, male role models describe their childhood reading experiences to encourage boys to read more. In Australia, a study found that providing positive male role models who read increased motivation and acceptance of reading among young male readers (Kelly, 2006).

Researchers including Michael W. Smith, Jeffrey Wilhelm, William Brozo, and Thomas Newkirk also are looking into what and why boys like to read. What they've discovered is that boys *do* read, but they are reading different forms of text. Also, educators and parents must pay attention to how boys *respond* to reading.

I have identified five major factors involved in successfully selecting books for boys: interest, choice, social factors, involvement, and text types (see figure below).

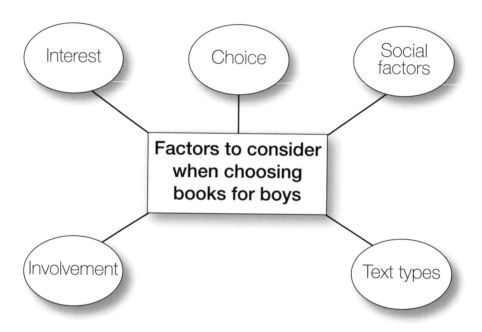

Interest

Boys have varied interests, and they can change as quickly as the weather. One day it may be sports; the next it could be cars, space, or dragons. It's vital to know boys' interests when helping them select books. My mother, a children's librarian, would ask, "What do you like?" when helping a young patron find books. This helped her to lead the child to titles he or she might enjoy.

Brozo describes this extensively in his book *To Be a Boy, to Be a Reader* (1999). He lists many ways to assess a boy's interests, including interest journals, book talks, and the well-known interest inventory. By determining children's interests, especially for outside-of-school reading, we can better match them with books they enjoy. Then teachers and parents must ensure that these texts (they are not always books) are accessible to children whether in the classroom, the library, or the home.

Choice

Humor, adventure, nonfiction, and sports. These genres appeal to boy readers, but often they are not accepted in the school setting.

Author Gordon Korman asks, "Why don't we value humor when we know it's what boys like?" (International Reading Association Conference, 2006). A good question. Perhaps the answer lies in the fact that humorous literature comes in shapes and sizes that are not deemed "book-like." Comic books, joke books, and series such as Dav Pilkey's Captain Underpants can be misunderstood and unappreciated. Yet as Korman points out, this is what boys like to read. And as I have found in my research (Zbaracki, 2003), these genres can "hook" readers, especially reluctant readers (those who can read but choose not to), and motivate them to explore other types of literature.

More and more nonfiction texts are being published. Publishers are hearing teachers' demands for nonfiction, which means that teachers are hearing their students, both boys and girls, request more of this genre.

There has been much discussion about crossover books (books that both boys and girls will read). However, what's been found is that girls will cross over into "boy books" much more than boys will cross over into "girl books." For example, *Olive's Ocean* by Kevin Henkes is an excellent book, and girls enjoy the story, but boys will not be as engaged with the "female issues" of love, a first kiss, and relationships with friends and family. Girls, however, will be just as engaged in an exciting adventure story, curious to see if the character will survive. Gary Paulsen's now-classic *Hatchet* is an example of this. Adventure books continue to be very popular with boys. Whether it be *Hatchet*, Will Hobbs's adventure novels such as *Far North* and *Crossing the Wire*, or Korman's On the Run series, the adventure book continues to attract new boy readers.

Social factors

Reading can be a very social activity among boys (Smith & Wilhelm, 2002). Often boys will find books to read based on peer recommendations. Many authors cite childhood role models who inspired them to read. It's important that boys have friends, family members, and teachers with whom they can talk about books. These interactions provide motivation for reading. Witness the Harry Potter phenomenon: Once a book becomes part of social discussion, it elevates in importance and this motivates readers, whether boys or girls.

Providing time for book discussions is one way to invite boys to tell others about the books they're enjoying. This validates their reading and provides an outlet for them to talk about their favorite titles, authors, and series.

Involvement

Too often in school, boys read only to complete assignments and take tests. Boys long to get involved in their reading (Smith & Wilhelm).

When planning curriculum, schools need to consider how they can keep boys involved in reading. As mentioned above, Smith and Wilhelm found that boys can view reading as too schoolish. They prefer their reading to be more purposeful — part of a real context. Brozo talks about giving boys some control over their responses to reading to keep them involved. Smith and Wilhelm also discuss this idea, suggesting drama as a method to get boys actively involved in reading. They have discovered that boys are eager "to get into the story," yet reluctant to engage with "school" reading.

Other techniques include using recent texts and matching classics with modern-day variations. *Romeo and Juliet* can be paired with Sharon M. Draper's modern-day version, *Romiette and Julio*. *The Great Gatsby* can be compared to Gordon Korman's creative *Jake Reinvented*.

Book discussion groups for boys encourage social involvement. Boys-only book clubs (reading books chosen by the boys themselves) have been found to be quite successful (Lingo, 2007; *School Library Journal,* 2007; Scieszka, 2005).

Text Types

As readers are exposed to more than books (magazines, newspapers, online resources, and electronic manuals, for example), it becomes more of a challenge to match readers with texts (Opitz, Ford, & Zbaracki, 2006). Those who help boys select books must be accepting of these new text structures.

As mentioned above, nonfiction is getting more attention in classrooms across the country. While states use nonfiction as reading selections on assessments, children are still taught primarily through narrative text. Boys can be set up for success on assessments when they are accustomed to reading and evaluating nonfiction. This is accomplished not by "teaching to the test" but by providing boys with access to a genre that already motivates them to read.

The rise of the graphic novel has many adults confused. With titles including Jeff Smith's Bone series, anything by Will Eisner, the recently published version of *Artemis Fowl,* or even Jon Scieszka's Time Warp Trio, graphic novels are here to stay. Some may consider these books to be glorified comics, and this new text type struggles to remain on library shelves across the country. The format of humorous text and graphic novels is discussed in *Books and Beyond* (Opitz, Ford, & Zbaracki, 2006). The authors stress that such an engaging genre must be accepted and accessible to readers, especially boys.

The books included in this volume were well received by male readers I have encountered — both in my teaching (of children and college students) and in casual discussions. When choosing titles I also based selections upon recommendations by public and school librarians, colleagues, and professional journals (*The Horn Book* and *The Reading Teacher* are examples). While a few of the selected titles have female protagonists, these tend to be exciting adventures featuring strong main char-

acters with universal appeal. The selection of books that follows will motivate and engage boys for years to come.

Sources

Brozo, W. (2002). *To Be a Boy, to Be a Reader*. Newark, DE: International
Reading Association.

Kelly, P. (2006). "Boys, Books, Blokes, and Bytes." *Aplis* 20(2) June,
72–83.

Korman, G. (2006). "Guys Write, Guys Read, and Guys Talk About
Reading." Presented at the International Reading Association
Conference, Chicago.

Lingo, S. (2007). "The All-Guys Book Club: Where Boys Take the Risk to
Read." *Library Media Connection* April/May, 24–28.

Newkirk, T. (2002). *Misreading Masculinity*. Portsmouth, NH:
Heinemann.

Opitz, M., Ford, M., & Zbaracki, M. (2006). *Books and Beyond*.
Portsmouth, NH: Heinemann.

School Library Journal (2007). September, 15.

Scieszka, J. (editor) (2005). *Guys Write for Guys Read*. New York: Viking.

Smith, W. & Wilhelm, J. (2002). *Reading Don't Fix No Chevys*.
Portsmouth, NH: Heinemann.

Zbaracki, M. (2003). A Descriptive Study of How Humorous Children's
Literature Serves to Engage Children in Reading. Ph.D. diss., The
Ohio State University, Columbus, OH.

Chapter 2

Humor

Humorous books engage young readers, especially reluctant readers. This genre can transform an unenthusiastic reader into an avid one.

This chapter begins with picture books. Boys will read and reread these titles (with their parents' help) as they get caught up in the world of books. They will establish a firm grasp on their interests and move on to the chapter books and novels also included in this chapter. One of the authors I have used most successfully in my teaching is Gordon Korman. His style and sense of humor have appealed to many of the male readers with whom I have worked.

Start with the books listed in this chapter and see if you don't get boys hooked on reading. This chapter is divided into three sections: Picture Books, Novels, and Short Stories.

Picture Books

1   **Agee, Jon. *Smart Feller, Fart Smeller: And Other Spoonerisms.***
    Hyperion, 2006, ISBN 0-7868-3692-X. 64p. ■ **Grades 3–5**
The title alone will draw male readers into this excellent wordplay book. Riddles are answered with "spoonerisms" (funny mix-ups of words or the initial sounds of words). For example, "What did the

trucker order for lunch? A chilled grease sandwich." There is an answer key at the back of the book to help readers decipher the trickier ones.

2   Arnold, Tedd. *Even More Parts.*
Dial, 2004, ISBN 978-0-8037-2938-4. 40p. ▪ **Grades 2–4**

The idioms continue in this sequel to *Parts* and *More Parts* (see below). Each page has more word play on different body parts and expressions. Readers will laugh at both the illustrations and the text.

3   Arnold, Tedd. *More Parts.*
Dial, 2001, ISBN 978-0-8037-1417-5. 32p. ▪ **Grades 2–4**

The boy with the body that was falling apart is back. This time he's found out about idioms, and uses them the best he can. The mixed-up idioms and Arnold's illustrations combine for a comical result. A great book for learning vocabulary and language.

4   Arnold, Tedd. *Parts.*
Dial, 1997, ISBN 978-0-8037-2040-4. 32p. ▪ **Grades 2–4**

What happens when you think your body is falling apart? Ear wax, loose teeth and other bodily phenomena alarm an imaginative young boy. The humorous illustrations and rhyming text will have readers laughing and wanting more, which they will find in the two sequels (see above).

5   Bateman, Teresa. *Keeper of Soles.*
Ill. by Yayo. Holiday House, 2008, ISBN 978-0-8234-2137-4. 30p. ▪ **Grades 2–4**

Colin is an expert shoemaker. When the Grim Reaper comes knocking, Colin does some quick thinking and sees the Grim Reaper needs some new shoes. Again and again the Grim Reaper returns for Colin only to have Colin make a new pair of shoes. When the Grim Reaper says enough is enough, Colin tells him he's given him plenty of soles. The humor and creativity of this story will have readers laughing and cheering for Colin's smart thinking.

6   Bloom, Suzanne. *A Splendid Friend, Indeed.*
Boyds Mills, 2005, ISBN 978-1-59078-286-6. 32p.
▪ **Grades 2–3**
✪ **Theodor Seuss Geisel Honor Book**

A simple but beautiful story accompanied by beautiful illustrations.
Bear is reading and writing, and Goose insists on talking to him the
whole time. Can a friendship develop from this? This absolutely
delightful tale is ideal for reading aloud. There is a sequel to this
book, *Treasure* (2007).

7   Carroll, Lewis. *Jabberwocky.*
Ill. by Christopher Myers. Jump at the Sun, 2007, ISBN 978-
1-4231-0372-1. 32p. ▪ **Grades 3–5**

Myers takes the reader on a modern-day version of Carroll's *Jabberwocky*. In this book the setting is the basketball court, and the Jab-
berwock is a brute on the court. The illustrations are fabulous and
boys will love this "sports version" of a classic poem.

8   Cronin, Doreen. *Click, Clack, Moo: Cows that Type.*
Ill. by Betsy Lewin. Simon & Schuster, 2000, ISBN 978-0-
689-83213-0. 32p. ▪ **Grades 2–4**

When the cows find an old typewriter, everything on the farm
changes. The cows demand electric blankets for themselves and
even for the chickens. A negotiation takes place between Farmer
Brown and the cows with Duck acting as the neutral party. A very
funny barnyard story. The two other books in the series are *Duck for
President* and *Giggle, Giggle, Quack* (see below).

9   Cronin, Doreen. *Diary of a Worm.*
Ill. by Harry Bliss. Joanna Cotler Books, 2003, ISBN 978-0-
06-000150-6. 40p. ▪ **Grades 2–4**

True to its title, this book, in diary format, is all about the life of a
worm. He describes his family, his friends, and even his school.
Bliss's illustrations add to the book's appeal. Two other books in the
series may interest fans of this book: *Diary of a Spider* (2005) and
Diary of a Fly (2007).

10   Cronin, Doreen. *Duck for President.*
Ill. by Betsy Lewin. Simon & Schuster, 2004, ISBN 978-0-689-86377-6. 32p. ▪ Grades 2–4

Duck wants a kinder, gentler farm, so he holds an election to oust Farmer Brown. He then successfully runs for governor and even president. In the end, Duck returns to the farm and decides to write his autobiography. A very funny tongue-in-cheek look at the election process.

11   Cronin, Doreen. *Giggle, Giggle, Quack.*
Ill. by Betsy Lewin. Simon & Schuster, 2002, ISBN 0-439-52153-X. 32p. ▪ Grades 2–4

Problems arise when Farmer Brown goes on vacation and leaves his brother Bob in charge. Duck finds a pencil, and his notes to Bob include some unusual demands. Farmer Brown's vacation is cut short when he must come home and fix what Duck has done to the farm.

12   Cronin, Doreen. *Thump, Quack, Moo: A Whacky Adventure.*
Ill. by Betsy Lewin. Atheneum, 2008, ISBN 978-1-4169-1630-7. 42p. ▪ Grades 2–3

Duck and Farmer are back! Now they're building corn mazes. Readers will enjoy seeing Duck and Farmer Brown back on the farm as they embark on a new adventure.

13   Danziger, Paula. *Barfburger Baby, I Was Here First.*
Ill. by G. Brian Karas. Putnam, 2004, ISBN 978-0-399-23204-6. 32p. ▪ Grades 2–4

Jonathan's not too crazy about his new baby brother and all the attention he gets. Jonathan makes up all sorts of nicknames for his brother, including "Barfburger Baby." But when family and friends come to visit, Jonathan learns that maybe it's OK to have a little brother.

14   Eaton, Jason. *The Day My Runny Nose Ran Away.*

Ill. by Ethan Long. Dutton, 2002, ISBN 978-0-525-47013-7. 32p. ▪ Grades 3–5

One day Jason wakes up to find a note from his nose. His nose is upset about how it has been treated and has run away. Jason realizes how important his nose is and when he sets out to find it, he stumbles upon a nose rebellion.

15   Keller, Laurie. *Arnie the Doughnut.*

Holt, 2003, ISBN 978-0-8050-6283-0. 32p. ▪ Grades 3–5

The amazing adventure of a doughnut who learns that his fate is to be eaten. A bond forms between Arnie and Mr. Bing, the man who buys him. Readers will love the detailed pictures and the jokes. Boys will be hungry for doughnuts after finishing this book, which also makes a great read-aloud.

16   Kontis, Alethea. *Alpha Oops! The Day Z Went First.*

Ill. by Bob Kolar. Candlewick, 2006, ISBN 978-0-7636-2728-7. 48p. ▪ Grades 2–3

Who said the Z always needs to come last? In this twist on an alphabet book the Z decides he's had enough and heads straight to the front of the alphabet. This throws all the other letters for a loop. This is an alphabet book with an attitude that will leave readers laughing at the antics.

17   Kotzwinkle, William, and Glenn Murray. *Walter the Farting Dog.*

Ill. by Audrey Colman. Frog Ltd., 2001, ISBN 978-1-58394-053-2. 32p. ▪ Grades 3–5

Walter has a serious problem, and the title gives readers a clue. While Walter's family tries everything to help him, he continues to have farting issues. Boys will love all the attempts to help Walter, and the fact that his farting actually saves the day. Other books in this series include: *Walter the Farting Dog: Trouble at the Yard Sale*

(2004), *Walter the Farting Dog Goes on a Cruise* (2006), and *Walter the Farting Dog: Banned from the Beach* (2007).

18   Lester, Helen. *Tacky the Penguin.*
Ill. by Lynn Munsinger. Houghton Mifflin, 1988, ISBN 978-0-395-56233-8. 32p. ▪ **Grades 3–5**

A penguin that wears a Hawaiian shirt and bow tie? That's Tacky for you. Tacky truly is an odd bird, but he's nice to have around because he often saves the day. Though this book has been around for a while, it's quite funny and will have boys laughing at Tacky's crazy antics. There are many other Tacky books, including *Three Cheers for Tacky, Tacky in Trouble, Tacky and Emperor, Tacky and the Winter Games*, and *Tackylocks and the Three Bears*.

19   Long, Melinda. *Pirates Don't Change Diapers.*
Ill. by David Shannon. Harcourt, 2007, ISBN 978-0-15-205353-6. 44p. ▪ **Grades 2–3**

In this sequel to *How I Became a Pirate*, Jeremy Jacob is reunited with the captain of the pirate ship he met in the first book. Jeremy learns more about pirates, including that they don't baby-sit and they don't change diapers. A fun story combined with wonderful illustrations by David Shannon make for a very successful book.

20   McMullan, Kate, and Jim McMullan. *I Stink!*
Joanna Cotler Books, 2002, ISBN 978-0-06-029848-7. 32p. ▪ **Grades 2–4**

A day in the life of a garbage truck. Boys will love the yucky alphabet soup that the garbage truck gobbles down. This is a great read-aloud: the truck is the narrator, and he has quite a way with words.

21   Palatini, Margie. *The Web Files.*
Ill. by Richard Egielski. Hyperion, 2001, ISBN 978-0-7868-0419-1. 32p. ▪ **Grades 3–5**

A crime has been committed down on the farm! Ducktective Web must try to solve the case. Through wordplay, tongue-twisters, and numerous references to nursery rhymes and pop culture, the crime is finally solved. Readers will love this book's humor — and enjoy trying to read the tough tongue-twisters aloud.

22 Pilkey, Dav. *Dog Breath: The Horrible Trouble with Hally Tosis.*

Scholastic, 1994, ISBN 0-590-69818-4. 32p. ▪ **Grades 3–5**

Hally Tosis is a dog with chronic bad breath. Nothing her owners do to help Hally with her breath problem works. In the end, though, Hally's bad breath helps save the day, making her a hero. This is a very funny tale, full of clever puns. Comparisons can be made between this book and *Walter the Farting Dog* (see entry 17), but this book was written first and is much more original and clever.

23 Scieszka, Jon. *Cowboy and Octopus.*

Ill. by Lane Smith. Viking, 2007, ISBN 978-0-670-91058-8. 40p. ▪ **Grades 2–4**

Cowboy and Octopus are two very unlikely friends. But together they make a teeter-totter work, shake hands . . . and hands . . . and hands (a total of eight times), go trick-or-treating, and enjoy other funny adventures. Readers who like other books by Scieszka and Smith will howl with laughter. The cut-paper artwork adds to the book's appeal.

24 Scieszka, Jon. *Seen Art?*

Ill. by Lane Smith. Viking, 2005, ISBN 978-0-670-05986-7. 48p. ▪ **Grades 3–6**

In search of his friend Art, a young boy finds himself being introduced to many of the great works in the Museum of Modern Art before he finally finds his friend waiting outside. The many misunderstandings and the comical illustrations add to the fun.

25 Shannon, David. *David Gets in Trouble.*

Blue Sky Press, 2002, ISBN 978-0-439-05022-7. 32p. ▪ **Grades 1–3**

This third book about David (after *No, David* and *David Goes to School*) shares the limited text of the earlier ones but is a bit more complex as it relates David's various missteps and the elaborate excuses he comes up with. The pictures of David's zany acts will attract readers.

26   Shannon, David. *Duck on a Bike.*
Blue Sky Press, 2002, ISBN 978-0-439-05023-4. 32p.
▪ Grades 2–3

Whoever heard of a duck riding a bike? David Shannon has created a hysterically funny book about what happens when a duck rides a bike and all the other barnyard animals join in the fun. The illustrations are vivid and comical, and invite young readers to greet the duck as he rides by.

27   Shulman, Mark. *A Is for Zebra.*
Ill. by Tamara Petrosino. Sterling, 2006, ISBN 978-1-4027-3494-6. 32p. ▪ Grades 3–4

This is a fun alphabet book that plays with words. "A is for zebrA" and "Z is for JazZ" provide a clue of how the book works. Readers will enjoy the challenging and creative plays with words. The illustrations will keep them entertained as well.

28   Simms, Laura. *Rotten Teeth.*
Ill. by David Catrow. Sandpiper, 1998, ISBN 978-0-618-25078-3. 32p. ▪ Grades 2–4

Melissa Hermann believes her house is boring and there's nothing interesting enough to take to school for show-and-tell. Catrow's great illustrations clearly show that the opposite is true. Melissa's brother Norman suggests a jar of the rotten teeth from their dentist father's office, and show-and-tell in Melissa's class will never be the same! The illustrations add to the humor of the book.

29   Smith, Lane. *The Happy Hocky Family.*
Viking, 1993, ISBN 978-0-670-85206-2. 64p. ▪ Grades 2–3

Meet the Hocky family! They have a somewhat strange sense of humor. Short stories about the family contain funny excerpts about their life. The humor — about burst balloons, oversmelly perfume, clothes shrunk in the wash — pokes fun at the family members and at childhood itself. The simplistic yet detailed drawings add to the enjoyment. Boys who like this book can also try *The Happy Hocky Family Moves to the Country.*

30 **Teague, Mark.** *LaRue for Mayor: Letters from the Campaign Trail*

Blue Sky Press, 2008, ISBN 978-0-439-78315-6. 32p.
- Grades 2–4

Ike the dog is at it again! This time he decides to run for mayor when he finds out that the current mayor is running on a platform of cracking down on free-roaming dogs. When Ike saves the mayor, the official must rethink his platform. Fans of *Dear Mrs. LaRue* and *Detective LaRue* will be excited to see a new title with Ike.

31 **Willems, Mo.** *Don't Let the Pigeon Drive the Bus!*

Hyperion, 2003, ISBN 978-0-7868-1988-1. 32p.
- Grades 1–3

Pigeon has a dream: to drive the bus. The bus driver leaves careful instructions against this, but Pigeon tries his best anyway. Each page will have young readers laughing and telling the pigeon, "No, no, no!" Other pigeon books include *Don't Let the Pigeon Stay Up Late* (see below), *Pigeon Finds a Hot Dog*, and *The Pigeon Has Feelings Too*.

32 **Willems, Mo.** *Don't Let the Pigeon Stay Up Late.*

Hyperion, 2006, ISBN 0-7868-3746-2. 36p. ▪ Grades 1–3

Pigeon tries his best to stay up late, as all children do. Readers will see many similarities in format to the other Pigeon books. Very observant readers will also pick out characters from other books by Mo Willems.

Novels

33 **Avi, and Rachel Vail.** *Nevermind: A Twin Novel.*

HarperTrophy, 2005, ISBN 978-0-06-054316-7. 208p.
- Grades 5–7

Twins Edward and Meg are seventh-graders of opposite extremes. Meg is the family overachiever, while Edward is the classic underachiever who attends an "alternative" school. Embarrassed by

Edward, Meg creates a fictional "dream" brother who all her friends fall in love with — sight unseen. For fun, and perhaps even to help Meg out, Edward tries to be that dream brother, even putting together a band to play at a party for his sister's friends. The band's first (and only) concert makes for a funny evening, and the twins learn they just may be able to coexist. Readers learn both sides of the story as the twins take turns narrating the chapters.

34   Bauer, Michael Gerard. *Don't Call Me Ishmael.*
HarperTeen, 2007, ISBN 978-0-06-134834-1. 272p.
- **Grades 7–9**

Ninth-grader Ishmael Leseur knew it was just a matter of time before class bully Barry Bagsley created yet another derogatory nickname for him. But his new English teacher and a new student, James Scobie, make Ishmael's life a bit more interesting. Through his friendship with James, Ishmael is able to come out of his shell and stand up to Barry. The incidents of the class bully getting his own are hysterical, and Ishmael has a few comical run-ins with his dream girl.

35   Clements, Andrew. *Frindle.*
Simon & Schuster, 1996, ISBN 978-0-689-80669-8. 112p.
- **Grades 3–5**

Nick has a talent for getting his class out of homework assignments. But he has met his match in his fifth-grade teacher, Mrs. Granger (aka the Lone Granger). Frustrated by his lack of success, he asks her how words make it into the dictionary. This starts a word war, and Nick decides to substitute the word "frindle" for "pen." His word takes off nationwide and even makes it into the dictionary. Finally we find out how Mrs. Granger feels about the new word. This is a fast-paced story that has fun with words.

36   Erickson, John. *Hank the Cowdog: The Case of the Booby-Trapped Pickup.*
Putnam, 2007 pap., ISBN 978-0-14-240755-4. 130p. **Series: Hank the Cowdog.** - **Grades 3–4**

This is the forty-ninth book in the Hank the Cowdog series for early chapter-book readers. In this mystery Hank has his usual mishaps on the farm. When his owner, Slim, ends up with a new pickup truck on loan, Hank learns the hard way that the truck has magic powers. Younger readers will enjoy reading about Hank's predicaments.

37   Hiaasen, Carl. *Hoot.*

Knopf, 2002, ISBN 978-0-375-82181-3. 304p. ▪ **Grades 4–6**
❂ **Newbery Honor Book**

Roy Eberhardt finds himself the new kid yet again when his family is uprooted from Montana and sent to hot and humid Florida. Being the new kid is the same as always: having no friends, sitting alone at lunch, and being picked on. But when Roy follows "the running boy," his life changes. He stumbles upon an ecological cause and joins the fight to prevent a nesting ground for animals from becoming a pancake house. Many humorous incidents make this book a real hoot for boy readers.

38   Kinney, Jeff. *Diary of a Wimpy Kid.*

Abrams Books for Young Readers, 2007, ISBN 978-0-8109-9313-6. 224p. ▪ **Grades 5–8**

Greg Heffley is a middle-school boy whose mother forces him to keep a diary. In the diary he describes what happens in each day of his life. The entries also includes his comic creations. Male readers will find themselves relating well to Greg's struggles with middle school. The text and comic illustrations throughout will captivate readers. There are two other books in the series: *Diary of a Wimpy Kid: Rodrick Rules* and *Diary of a Wimpy Kid: A Survival Guide.*

39   Korman, Gordon. *Born to Rock.*

Hyperion, 2006, ISBN 978-0-7868-0920-2. 261p.
▪ **Grades 9–12**

Young Republican Club president and high school senior Leo Carraway loses his scholarship to Harvard — and his hope of attending the school of his dreams. When he learns that his biological father is the lead singer of a famous punk-rock band, he's even more confused. He and his ultra-liberal best friend, Melinda, decide he should tour with his father's band as a roadie. During a wild summer on tour, Leo learns about punk music, discovers his feelings for his best friend, and finds out secrets about his father that help him come to terms with where he'll attend college.

40   Korman, Gordon. *The Chicken Doesn't Skate.*
Hyperion, 1998, ISBN 978-0-590-85301-9. 197p.
- Grades 4–6

Sixth-grader Milo Neal comes up with an excellent project for the school science fair: the life cycle of a chicken. Unexpectedly, his project becomes the mascot of the hockey team and cures their slump. Milo's classmates take turns telling this story that ends when the students learn that the life cycle ends when the chicken is eaten.

41   Korman, Gordon. *Maxx Comedy.*
Hyperion, 2003, ISBN 978-0-7868-0746-8. 160p.
- Grades 4–6

Sixth-grader Max Carmody believes he's the funniest kid in America, and he tries to prove it by telling jokes to anyone who will listen. When he sees a flyer for a contest seeking the funniest kid in America, he signs up and asks his friends to help him make a winning videotape. Each attempt backfires until Max's patient and loving stepfather helps him get a shot at the big time.

42   Korman, Gordon. *No More Dead Dogs.*
Hyperion, 2000, ISBN 978-0-7868-0531-0. 192p.
- Grades 5–8

Eighth-grader Wallace Wallace cannot lie, so when he reads his English teacher's favorite book (*Old Shep, My Pal*) and writes his book report, he gives an honest assessment: it stinks. Wallace has learned that if a book has a dog on the cover and an award as well, the dog is going to die. His English teacher puts him in detention until he writes a favorable review of the book. Wallace ends up rewriting the script of the school play (which happens to be based on *Old Shep*) as a rock musical. True to Korman's signature style, the events build to a hysterical climax.

43   Korman, Gordon. *Schooled.*

Hyperion, 2007, ISBN 978-0-7868-5692-3. 224p.
- Grades 6–8

Fourteen-year-old Capricorn Anderson has lived his life so far on a commune with his still-hippie grandmother. While other hippies have joined the twenty-first century, Capricorn's grandmother fights change. When she has an accident that puts her in the hospital, previously home-schooled Capricorn must attend public school while staying with a very understanding social worker and her family. Things don't go well at Capricorn's new school when some popular students try to make him the school joke. But Capricorn's ignorance of social norms soon makes him the most popular boy in the school. Each day is funnier as Capricorn unknowingly outwits his prankster classmates.

44   Korman, Gordon. *The Sixth Grade Nickname Game.*

Hyperion, 1999, ISBN 978-0-7868-0432-0. 144p.
- Grades 5–7

Sixth-graders Wiley and Jeff are best friends and nickname kings. They can give anyone a nickname and make it stick. They were even able to win a bet by giving the blandest boy in school a cool nickname. But when a new girl joins their class, the boys struggle for her nickname, and even begin to question their friendship. With the help of their new teacher, a whistle-blowing football coach, the boys learn about life, reading, and each other.

45   Korman, Gordon. *Son of the Mob.*

Hyperion, 2002, ISBN 978-0-7868-0769-7. 272p.
- Grades 7–11

Seventeen-year-old Vince Luca is the son of a mob kingpin. He falls in love with a girl in his school who happens to be the daughter of the FBI agent assigned to bring down Vince's father. Keeping the relationship a secret from his family proves quite challenging. The fact that Vince wants nothing to do with the Mafia connections he's grown up with adds to the humor of the story. Fans of this book can check out the sequel: *Son of the Mob: Hollywood Hustle* (see below).

46   Korman, Gordon. *Son of the Mob: Hollywood Hustle.*
Hyperion, 2004, ISBN 978-0-7868-0918-9. 268p.
  ▪ **Grades 7–11**

Vince Luca is back, and so is his girlfriend, the daughter of the FBI agent assigned to bring down Vince's Mafia kingpin father. This time both Vince and his girlfriend are off to California to attend college. Vince longs to be a great filmmaker. But when his father's "business" decides to set up shop on the West Coast, Vince's life is turned upside down, and his relationship with his girlfriend begins to change as well. Now Vince must try to disconnect from his father and at the same time do well in his classes and reconnect with his girlfriend.

47   Korman, Gordon. *Why Did the Underwear Cross the Road?*
Apple, 1997, ISBN 978-0-590-47502-0. 112p. ▪ **Grades 3–5**

The three Zs are fourth-graders who want to win the school good-deed contest. Justin Zechendorf declares himself their "idea man." But all his ideas backfire and cause more problems for the team. In true Korman style, the three Zs win the good-deed contest and solve a crime at the same time.

48   Lubar, David. *Punished!*
Darby Creek, 2005, ISBN 978-1-58196-042-6. 96p.
  ▪ **Grades 3–5**

Logan is horsing around in the library with his friend when he crashes into Professor Wordsworth. His punishment? He may speak only in puns unless he's able to find seven palindromes, anagrams, and oxymorons in three days. This leaves Logan frantically playing with words, and the reader learning about the fun to be had with language.

49 **Lubar, David.** *Sleeping Freshmen Never Lie.*
Dutton, 2005, ISBN 978-0-525-47311-4. 160p.
- **Grades 7–10**

Scott Hudson is a typical high school freshman. He's small and easy prey for the seniors. While Scott struggles to adapt to high school he decides to pursue the girl of his dreams by joining every school activity she's in. But each attempt backfires. Even more hilarity ensues when the school delinquent befriends Scott. In the end Scott learns the ins and outs of surviving — and possibly even enjoying — high school.

50 **Pilkey, Dav.** *The Adventures of Captain Underpants.*
Blue Sky Press, 1997, ISBN 978-0-590-84627-1. 128p.
- **Grades 3–5**

Fourth-graders George and Harold create their own superhero by using a 3-D Hypno-ring to turn their principal into Captain Underpants. Each book in this series uses gross-out humor, wordplay, the infamous flip-o-rama, and a comic-book style. Adults may not approve of these books, but boys flock to them for their humor. Let them read and reread them as springboards to other humor titles. Other titles in the series include: *Captain Underpants and the Attack of the Talking Toilets, Captain Underpants and the Invasion of the Incredibly Naughty Cafeteria Ladies from Outer Space, Captain Underpants and the Perilous Plot of Professor Poopypants*, and *Captain Underpants and the Wrath of the Wicked Wedgie Woman*.

51 **Riddleburger, Sam.** *The Qwikpick Adventure Society.*
Dial, 2007, ISBN 978-0-8037-3178-3. 127p. ▪ **Grades 4–6**

Lyle Hertzog and his friends Marilla and Dave decide to spend their Christmas on an adventure. They journey to visit the amazing fountain of poop at a nearby sewage plant. While it's not a wild adventure, the Qwikpick Adventure Society members do end up at the fountain of poop, and one of them gets a bit too close. Any book with a poop fountain will appeal to boys, and this quick read will engage them.

52   Scieszka, Jon. *Knights of the Kitchen Table.*
Ill. by Lane Smith. Viking, 1991, ISBN 978-0-670-83622-2.
64p. ▪ **Grades 3–5**

In the first book in the Time Warp Trio series, narrator Joe is given a book that takes him through time. In this installment, he and his friends Fred and Sam travel back to King Arthur's day, where they must search for the book that will send them back to the present. Scieszka and Smith create humorous scenes in each time period. This is a great series to motivate boy readers. Other titles include *The Good, the Bad, and the Goofy*; *It's All Greek to Me*; *The Not So Jolly Roger*; *See You Later Gladiator*; *Summer Reading Is Killing Me*; *Tut Tut*; *2095*; *Your Mother Was a Neanderthal*; and *Sam Samurai*.

Short Stories

53   Scieszka, Jon. *Guys Write for Guys Read.*
Viking, 2005, ISBN 0-670-06007-0. 272p. ▪ **Grades 5–12**

Scieszka has collected stories from many male writers and illustrators. Each one is about what it's like to be a boy and to love reading and writing. Some of the stories are hysterically funny and will make readers laugh out loud. Each author also recommends a few of his favorite books. This is a great collection of stories that will help boys realize that they are not alone — and that promotes the importance of reading in boys' lives.

Chapter 3

Realistic Fiction

I t has been said that realistic fiction "reassures young people that they are not the first in the world to have faced problems" (Kiefer, Hepler, Hickman, 2006). This is true for both boys *and* girls, whether the problems are at home, at school, or with friends. At the same time, by reading realistic fiction young adults may be exposed to issues and situations that they have not yet experienced.

This chapter includes separate sections on sports stories and adventure stories. While realistic fiction titles are available for many age levels, there are some particularly exceptional books for young adult readers. I strongly encourage you to seek out these titles and to recommend them to young adult male readers. This chapter is divided into three sections: General Realistic Fiction, Adventure Stories, and Sports Stories (subdivided into Picture Books and Novels).

General Realistic Fiction

54   Adoff, Jaime. *Jimi and Me.*
Jump at the Sun, 2005, ISBN 978-0-7868-5214-7. 336p.
- Grades 7–9
- ✪ Coretta Scott King New Talent Award

Don't let the length of this book scare off your boy readers. This novel, written in poetic form, tells the story of thirteen-year-old

Keith, a boy of mixed race, as he deals with the unexpected death of his father. As the money disappears, Keith and his mother are forced to move in with Keith's aunt in a small Ohio town. Used to the pace of New York City, Keith struggles with this change and learns secrets about his father.

55   Alexie, Sherman. *Absolutely True Diary of a Part-Time Indian.*
Little, Brown, 2007, ISBN 978-0-316-01368-0. 240p.
- Grades 7–12

Arnold Spirit is a 14-year-old Indian (Native American) struggling with his identity. When he transfers from his school on the reservation to a new, rich white school he makes new friends and even becomes a starter on the basketball team. When his new school plays his old school, identity issues abound along with the many challenges Arnold faces in his home life as well. Alexie's humor engages the reader and provides comic relief from some of Arnold's struggles.

56   Anderson, Laurie Halse. *Twisted.*
Viking, 2007, ISBN 978-0-670-06101-3. 272p.
- Grades 9–12

Tyler Miller is ready for a great senior year of high school. He has just spent the summer doing manual labor as community service for a graffiti prank gone wrong. He is newly popular at school, thanks to the physique and the bad-boy reputation he developed over the summer. Even better, the girl of his dreams, Bethany Milbury, is attracted to Tyler. Bethany invites him to a party that gets out of control and gets Tyler in deep trouble . . . leaving him desperate to restore his good name. This is another powerful and suspenseful novel by Anderson; it could be paired with one of her earlier novels, *Speak*.

57   Brooks, Kevin. *Lucas.*
Chicken House, 2003, ISBN 978-0-439-45698-2. 432p.
- Grades 9–12

Fifteen-year-old Caitlin tells this story about sixteen-year-old Lucas and his arrival in her small town in Great Britain. Lucas is very much

an independent thinker, living off the land and not disturbing anyone. This starts to make people uncomfortable, especially the town's
drunk and rowdy college boys. When a girl is assaulted, all eyes turn
to the mysterious stranger, and Lucas's life is in danger. This gripping
novel will provoke discussion.

58   Cottrell Boyce, Frank. *Framed.*

HarperCollins, 2006, ISBN 978-0-06-073402-2. 320p.
- Grades 4–6

Dylan Hughes thinks the dreary Welsh town of Manod is beautiful.
His family runs the local garage, but when business slows his father
leaves. This means Dylan, his mother, and his two sisters must try to
run the garage until he comes back, if he ever does. At the same
time flooding in London forces the National Gallery to bring its
paintings to the mine in Manod for safekeeping. The curator thinks
Dylan is an art lover when he hears the names of Dylan's chickens
(Donatello and Michelangelo, actually named after the Teenage
Mutant Ninja Turtles). Dylan's sister Minnie hatches a scheme to
steal one of the paintings. Humor abounds and the town starts to
change, all because of the artwork. Another creative story from
Boyce.

59   Cottrell Boyce, Frank. *Millions.*

HarperCollins, 2004, ISBN 978-0-06-073330-8. 256p.
- Grades 4–7

Damian finds a bag full of cash by the railroad tracks near his new
house. The bag is full of British pounds, which in two short weeks
will no longer be used since they're being replaced by euros. Damian and his brother see this as a reason to start spending the money as
soon as possible. But they run into problems, primarily that Damian
wants to be charitable with the money and his brother wants to make
more with it. This leads to many funny twists and turns, and in the
end the boys learn about the value of money while dealing with the
loss of their mother. Readers will enjoy considering what they would
do in the same situation.

60   Creech, Sharon. *Hate That Cat.*
HarperCollins, 2008 forthcoming. ▪ **Grades 5–8**

Jack is back, and so is Mrs. Stretchberry! In this sequel to *Love that Dog* (see below) Jack and his teacher continue to delve into the world of poetry.

61   Creech, Sharon. *Love That Dog.*
HarperCollins, 2000, ISBN 0-06-029287-3. 86p.
▪ **Grades 5–7**

Jack hates poetry. He doesn't like to read it or write it. (When forced to, he writes, "Boys / don't write poetry. / Girls do.") Then his teacher introduces him to poems and poets, especially Walter Dean Myers, and his love of poetry begins. Soon he begins to write his own poems and even tells his teacher it's okay if they're read aloud to the class. This book is written in Jack's voice, in poetic form. This is a must-read for any boy who has the slightest interest in poetry or in Walter Dean Myers.

62   Creech, Sharon. *Replay.*
Joanna Cotler Books, 2005, ISBN 978-0-06-054019-7. 240p.
▪ **Grades 5–7**

Leo is a middle child who finds himself overshadowed by his more outgoing siblings, earning him the family nickname "Sardine." Leo doesn't really know where he fits in — in his family or in life. When the school drama teacher puts on a play called *Rumpopo's Porch*, Leo finds himself cast in the drama. At the same time Leo finds a journal written by his father when he was thirteen years old. Leo discovers he is more like his father than he realized — and also that he can learn something from his role in the play. The text of the play, also written by Creech, is included in the book.

63   deGuzman, Michael. *Beekman's Big Deal.*
Farrar, Straus & Giroux, 2004, ISBN 0-374-30672-9. 213p.
▪ **Grades 4–6**

Beekman O'Day, who is twelve years old, is starting at his ninth school in New York City. He has the routine down pat: please the principal and try to make new friends. He hasn't gone through all these schools because he's a troublemaker; it's just that his father is always on the cusp of the next "big deal." Each time his dad can't pay the tuition, it's off to another school. Usually it's just when Beekman finally feels at home in each new school and house that his dad's dealmaking dries up. Is Beekman headed to his tenth school? Readers will be pulling for Beekman and turning pages to find out where he ends up next.

64   Draper, Sharon. *Romiette and Julio.*

Simon & Schuster, 2005 pap., ISBN 978-1-4169-1151-7. 336p. ▪ **Grades 7–10**

Julio Montaque is sixteen years old and has just moved to Cincinnati to escape the gangs in Texas. In an Internet chat room he meets Romiette Capelle, also sixteen and attending the same high school. It's easy to see the striking similarities between this couple and Romeo and Juliet, and that's the idea. In this modern-day version of the story, the interracial (Hispanic/African American) couple faces the disapproval of their classmates as well as their parents. A very suspenseful ending will have readers desperate to find out what happens. This could easily be paired with *Romeo and Juliet* for deeper discussions.

65   DuPrau, Jeanne. *Car Trouble.*

Greenwillow, 2005 pap., ISBN 978-0-06-073675-0. 274p. ▪ **Grades 9–12**

Duff has just graduated from high school and thinks he's got it made. He has a sweet computer job waiting for him in California. All he needs to do is drive there from his home in Virginia, and he's scheduled one week to do it. *Freedom! Adventure! Life!* thinks Duff. But when his car breaks down only a few hundred miles from home, Duff soon learns that even the best plans can fall apart. He must adjust and adapt as California seems farther away each day. This a very funny novel full of adventure and even romance as Duff meets a girl and is pursued by criminals.

66   Gantos, Jack. *Joey Pigza Swallowed the Key.*

Farrar, Straus & Giroux, 1998, ISBN 978-0-374-33664-6.
196p. Series: Joey Pigza. ▪ **Grades 4–6**

Joey Pigza is a wild child. He causes problems in school and is finally
sent to a special school after he accidentally injures a classmate.
There the teachers discover that Joey's medication for attention
deficit disorder (ADD) needs to be adjusted. Eventually he's allowed
back into his old school. Things look better for Joey, but it's still a
struggle for him to make good decisions and act on them. Told from
Joey's point of view, this is a good novel addressing the challenges
faced by children with ADD. Other books in the series include *Joey
Pigza Loses Control*, *What Would Joey Do?* and *I Am Not Joey
Pigza*.

**67   Glenn, Mel. *Who Killed Mr. Chippendale? A Mystery in
Poems.***

Putnam, 1999, ISBN 978-0-14-038513-7. 112p.
▪ **Grades 8–11**

A high school teacher is murdered, and the reader helps to determine who the guilty party is. The mystery is told through free verse
and presents the perspective of students, teachers, and other people
in the school. An epilogue describes where some of the characters
are thirteen years later.

68   Going, K. L. *Fat Kid Rules the World.*

Putnam, 2003, ISBN 0-399-23990-1. 187p. ▪ **Grades 8–11**
✪ **Michael L. Printz Honor Book**

This is an excellent first book by Going. Troy is overweight, unpopu-
lar, and contemplating suicide. He just can't think of a way to do it
without being laughed at after the fact. While he's standing on a
train platform, his classmate Curt talks him out of jumping and a
friendship develops. Curt is the best punk guitar player in the world
and a legend at the high school. Curt decides that Troy is the best
punk-rock drummer ever. The only problem is Troy has never played
drums in his life. Through many band practices and conversations,
Troy learns more about himself and about Curt — and decides that
maybe his life is pretty good after all.

69   Green, John. *Looking for Alaska.*
Dutton, 2005, ISBN 978-0-525-47506-4. 160p.
- Grades 9–12
- Michael L. Printz Award

Miles Halter is bored with his life in Florida. He decides to attend an elite boarding school in Alabama, thinking he'll make new friends and enjoy school more. At first he finds it's more of the same. But his roommate, Chip, and Chip's best friend, Alaska, teach Miles much about life. Miles is drawn to Alaska, but discovers she already has a boyfriend. Their friendship evolves during the school year and some wild behavior, and changes when tragedy strikes. This is a strong novel with Miles's humor sprinkled throughout.

70   Grimes, Nikki. *Bronx Masquerade.*
Dial, 2002, ISBN 0-8037-2569-8. 176p.   - Grades 8–11
- Coretta Scott King Author Award

Can an English teacher inspire inner-city high school students to write and read their own poetry? In this novel, one teacher is able to do just that. Through a monthly poetry slam, each character describes what's happening in his or her life, then writes a poem about the experience.

71   Henkes, Kevin. *The Birthday Room.*
Greenwillow, 1999, ISBN 978-0-688-16733-2. 152p.
- Grades 4–6

For Benjamin's twelfth birthday he receives two gifts. One is a new room (the old attic that has been redone) and the other is a letter from his uncle Ian inviting him to Oregon for a visit. Benjamin is very excited about the second gift because he has not seen his uncle since a woodworking accident that happened when Benjamin was two. During the visit Benjamin learns about his family and himself, and even decides what to do with his new room.

72   Henkes, Kevin. *Sun and Spoon.*
Greenwillow, 1997, ISBN 978-0-688-15232-1. 144p.
- Grades 3–5

Ten-year-old Spoon Gilmore's grandmother has just died. Spoon worries that he will forget her and the beautiful memories he has of her. He decides to steal an old set of her playing cards with suns on them as a way to remember her. He finds out that his grandfather also is looking for the cards as a memento. This brings the two of them closer as they remember Spoon's grandmother. A moving and beautifully written story.

73   **Hite, Sid.** *I'm Exploding Now.*
      Hyperion, 2007, ISBN 978-0-7868-3757-1. 192p.
      ▪ **Grades 6–9**

In diary format, Max Whooten describes his rough summer. At sixteen, he has no summer job, one friend who just got out of a mental institution and another who may also be the girl of his dreams. Worst of all he has a temper, and lately it's been showing itself a lot. When the family cat dies, Max escorts it from New York City to Woodstock, where his aunt has offered to bury the cat. Staying in Woodstock for a while helps Max to see that his life is actually pretty great, especially when he's introduced to Zini, a teenage artist who captures Max's eye and heart.

74   **Klass, David.** *You Don't Know Me.*
      HarperTeen, 2002 pap., ISBN 978-0-06-447378-1. 352p.
      ▪ **Grades 7–11**

John struggles to make himself "unknown" in school. If no one knows him, he reasons, he'll be able to sneak through life with no problems. Perhaps this stems from the abuse he suffers at the hands of his mother's live-in boyfriend. When the beatings escalate one night and John's life is truly in danger, he learns that he has not hidden himself as well as he thought, and perhaps that's a good thing. A well-written, potent novel.

75   **Kline, Suzy.** *Horrible Harry Cracks the Code.*
      Viking, 2007, ISBN 978-0-670-06200-3. 66p. **Series: Horrible Harry.** ▪ **Grades 2–3**

Horrible Harry is back, claiming to be the world's second-best detective (Sherlock Holmes being the first). This easier chapter book will build readers' confidence as they follow Harry in his efforts to solve a school cafeteria mystery. This is a good series for younger readers.

Other titles include *Horrible Harry and the Goog, Horrible Harry Goes to the Moon*, and *Horrible Harry Moves Up to Third Grade*.

76   Konigsburg, E. L. *Silent to the Bone.*
    Aladdin, 2002 pap., ISBN 978-0-689-83602-2. 261p.
    ▪ **Grades 5–7**

After thirteen-year-old Branwell Zamborska dials 911 to report that his baby sister is not breathing, he goes silent. His nanny comes on the phone and reports that Branwell dropped the baby. While his sister lies comatose and prosecutors debate about his future, the mute Branwell is sent to a home for troubled youth. His best friend, Connor, visits him frequently but Branwell remains silent. Connor devises a system using cards so Branwell can communicate. Using the information Branwell provides, as well as some help from his older stepsister, Connor is able to find out exactly what happened to Branwell and his baby sister. A creative story that will keep readers riveted.

77   Korman, Gordon. *Jake, Reinvented.*
    Hyperion, 2003, ISBN 0-7868-1957-X. 224p. ▪ **Grades 8–12**

Jake, originally a nerdy guy, changes his image and becomes a talented football player who throws wild beer bashes to attract the in crowd, and the girl of his dreams. Some, though, suspect there is more to Jake than meets the eye, and when his secret is revealed, Jake struggles to keep his new "cool" image from vanishing. There are wonderful comparisons to *The Great Gatsby* that savvy readers will pick up on.

78   Lubar, David. *Dunk.*
    Clarion, 2002, ISBN 978-0-618-19455-1. 256p.
    ▪ **Grades 8–11**

Chad is a teenager living near the boardwalk on the New Jersey shore. As summer approaches, he becomes fascinated by the "bozo" in the dunk tank. Thinking this would be a great way to work out his anger toward his deadbeat dad and his teachers, he signs up for the job. He soon learns that the work is much harder than it seems, but he's able to learn from a professional who's also a boarder in his house. The strategies he learns at the dunk tank help him deal with girls, bullies, and his best friend's illness. This excellent, humorous novel will capture the reader from the first chapter. Readers who enjoy this title will also like Lubar's *Sleeping Freshmen Never Lie* (entry 49).

79   Lynch, Chris. *Me, Dead Dad, and Alcatraz.*
HarperCollins, 2005, ISBN 978-0-06-059709-2. 240p.
- Grades 7–9

This is the third book about fourteen-year-old Elvin Bishop. He discovers that his dead uncle, Alex, isn't dead at all — he was just in prison. Now his uncle wants to make up for lost time and tries to become a father figure to Elvin. Readers who have already met Elvin and his buddies Mikie and Frankie will be happy to read more about them, though this book also stands well on its own. The first two books in the series are *Slot Machine* and *Extreme Elvin*.

80   Myers, Walter Dean. *Autobiography of My Dead Brother.*
Amistad, 2005, ISBN 978-0-06-058291-3. 224p.
- Grades 8–11
- ✪ National Book Award Finalist; ALA Best Book for Young Adults

Jesse lives in Harlem, New York. He's always idolized a neighbor two years older than he named Rise. Jesse, Rise, and a few other friends are in a social organization called the Counts. Recently Jesse has seen that Rise is pulling away from the Counts and from Jesse as well. Jesse struggles to understand this using the best outlet he has — art. The novel has black-and-white drawings and comic strip panels throughout. Readers will enjoy the artwork and be engaged by the story of what happens to Jesse and Rise.

81   Myers, Walter Dean. *Handbook for Boys.*
Amistad, 2002, ISBN 978-0-06-029146-4. 192p.
- Grades 8–11

After getting caught selling drugs, Jimmy is given a choice by a judge: do six months in a detention center or participate in a community mentoring program. Choosing the mentoring program, sixteen-year-old Jimmy works in Duke Wilson's barbershop with another troubled youth named Kevin. Each day after school Duke mentors them by pointing out the good and bad characteristics of each person who comes through the shop door. Through these stories Jimmy starts to learn more about the decisions he makes and where they might lead. Though this novel may seem preachy at times, it is intended to help boys choose the right paths in life.

82   **Myers, Walter Dean. *Monster*.**
      Amistad, 1999, ISBN 978-0-06-028077-2. 288p.
      ▪ **Grades 7–10**
      ✪ **Michael L. Printz Award, Coretta Scott King Honor Book**

Steve Harmon is on trial for murder because he acted as a lookout in a botched drugstore robbery that ended with the store owner's death. During Steve's trial, the prosecutors call him a "monster," and he's upset with the label. When he's told to write about his feelings, he does — in the form of a film script. This powerful story engages readers with its screenplay format.

83   **Myers, Walter Dean. *Shooter*.**
      Amistad, 2004, ISBN 978-0-06-029519-6. 224p.
      ▪ **Grades 8–11**

This novel about a high school shooting is told from the perspectives of those interviewing the friends of the killer. Each interview provides insights into how the shooting happened and whether it could have been prevented. This is a powerful novel that uses a creative approach. At the end of the book is the killer's "die-ary," which provides more insights for the reader. A strong young adult book addressing a serious issue.

84   **Myers, Walter Dean. *Street Love*.**
      Amistad, 2006, ISBN 978-0-06-028079-6. 144p.
      ▪ **Grades 8–12**

Damien is a seventeen-year-old basketball player and academic high achiever. He's been accepted to Brown University and has a bright future ahead of him. But when he starts dating Junice, a sixteen-year-old who's overprotective of her younger sister after her mother is jailed for drugs, Damien's parents begin to worry. This novel in verse tells Damien's story. Comparisons to *Romeo and Juliet* can be made with this book.

85   Paulsen, Gary. *The Amazing Life of Birds.*
Wendy Lamb Books, 2006, ISBN 0-385-74660-1. 84p.
■ Grades 6–8

Duane Harper Leech is a twelve-year-old who has just entered puberty. He struggles to work through the changes that his body is experiencing and decides to keep a journal to chronicle these changes. This humorous account tells about what happens each day and how he learns to cope. It will help other boys in this stage of life know that they're not alone.

86   Paulsen, Gary. *Lawn Boy.*
Wendy Lamb Books, 2007, ISBN 978-0-385-74686-1. 96p.
■ Grades 4–7

A boy gets his grandpa's old riding lawn mower and turns it into a very profitable summer job. Soon this twelve-year-old has his own business, employees, and stockbroker, and is even sponsoring a boxer. This quick read teaches business tips while providing plenty of laughs. Readers will be both amused and envious as they read about how much money the boy makes.

87   Sachar, Louis. *Holes.*
Farrar, Straus & Giroux, 1998, ISBN 978-0-374-33265-5.
240p. ■ Grades 4–6
✪ Newbery Medal

Stanley Yelnats is convicted of a crime he didn't commit. He's sure his family has been cursed with bad luck, and this is just another example of it. His sentence is to be served at Camp Green Lake, which is not a camp and has no lake. At Camp Green Lake he and the other boys must dig a hole each day. Stanley begins to learn the reason for all the digging. When one of Stanley's friends, Zero, runs off one day and Stanley goes to find him, they stumble upon the secret of Camp Green Lake. This award winner has been made into a movie. The sequel is *Small Steps* (see below).

88   Sachar, Louis. *Small Steps.*

Delacorte, 2006, ISBN 978-0-385-73314-4. 272p.
- **Grades 5–8**

This sequel to *Holes* focuses on Armpit, a former resident of Camp Green Lake. Armpit, now sixteen, is trying to leave his past behind but sometimes it catches up with him. When X-Ray (another "inmate" from Camp Green Lake) visits him with a get-rich proposition, Armpit takes the risk. The idea is to scalp tickets for the hottest show coming to town: Kaira DeLeon. With a couple of extra tickets Armpit takes his young neighbor Ginny to the show. They get to meet Kaira, and Kaira and Armpit begin a romance. This proves dangerous, and Armpit must save the day and his own life. Since this story does not rely much on knowledge of *Holes*, it can be read on its own.

89   Shannon, David. *Too Many Toys.*

Blue Sky Press, 2008, ISBN 978-0-439-49029-0. 32p.
- **Grades 2–4**

Spencer has a problem. He has too many toys. When his parents make him clean out his room and get rid of some of the old toys, he finds he can't make up his mind. Children who have been in the same situation as Spencer will be able to relate to the dilemma. Add to that Shannon's wonderful illustrations, and readers will be hooked.

90   Sonnenblick, Jordan. *Notes from the Midnight Driver.*

Scholastic, 2006, ISBN 0-439-75779-7. 265p. ▪ **Grades 8–11**

Sixteen-year-old Alex Gregory is having a hard time coping with his parents' divorce. One night he makes a horrible decision that lands him in jail. Alex receives a sentence of community service in a retirement home. His "assignment" is to befriend a cranky old man. What develops between Alex and his charge turns into a true friendship that changes the lives of everyone involved, especially Alex. Humorous elements add to the book's appeal.

91   Soto, Gary. *Crazy Weekend.*
Persea, 2003 pap., ISBN 978-0-89255-286-3. 160p.
- Grades 4–6

Seventh-graders Hector and Mando are from East Los Angeles. They decide to visit Hector's Uncle Julio, a photographer in Fresno, for the weekend. Unexpectedly, Uncle Julio ends up with photos of a bank robbery. The robbers find out that Hector and Mando were witnesses to the crime and set out to find them. Danger and humor collide as Hector and Mando continually outsmart the crooks. Spanish words are integrated into the text and there is a glossary at the end of the book. This is a paperback reissue of a 1994 publication.

92   Spinelli, Jerry. *Loser.*
HarperTrophy, 2002, ISBN 978-0-06-000193-3. 224p.
- Grades 4–6

Donald Zinkoff is unique and happy about it. He takes great pride in all he does and is oblivious to what others think. But when he enters fourth grade, other kids start to notice how different Zinkoff is, and he is labeled "Loser." Zinkoff stays true to himself and refuses to change, in the end proving himself not just unique but also courageous.

93   Spinelli, Jerry. *Stargirl.*
Knopf, 2000, ISBN 978-0-679-88637-2. 192p.
- Grades 7–10

Leo Borlock reflects on his junior year in high school in New Mexico. During that year he and his classmates became enamored with a formerly home-schooled student who goes by the name Stargirl. Stargirl is a nonconformist who sings "Happy Birthday" to people with her ukulele, wears a wedding dress to school, and even has a pet rat. She becomes very popular at the high school, but that brings a fall from grace. Leo is caught in the middle when he and Stargirl start to date. Leo learns he must decide what he values more: conformity or Stargirl. A sequel is *Love, Stargirl* (2007).

94   Spinelli, Jerry. *Wringer.*
Joanna Cotler Books, 1997, ISBN 978-0-06-024913-7. 240p.
- Grades 4–6

Palmer is about to turn ten. It's a tradition in his town that the ten-year-old boys wring the necks of pigeons at the town pigeon shoot. Palmer is sickened by this idea but his new friends are eager for their chance. Things get complicated when Palmer's friends discover that he's keeping a pigeon as a pet. Palmer is left with a choice: to give in to peer pressure and become a wringer, or to follow his own path. A well-told, powerful story.

95   Tashjian, Janet. *The Gospel According to Larry.*
Holt, 2001, ISBN 978-0-8050-6378-3. 192p. ▪ Grades 8–11

Josh is a high school senior in love with his next-door neighbor, Beth, but he's afraid to tell her how he feels. So instead he creates a fictional character, Larry, who has his own Web site. On this site he addresses issues and ideas that both he and Beth believe in. Beth is not the only one attracted to what Josh (disguised as Larry) is preaching. Soon a nationwide media circus forms over the mystery of Larry's true identity. When the truth comes out, Josh's life and his friendship with Beth change dramatically. There is a sequel: *Vote for Larry*.

96   Thomas, Rob. *Rats Saw God.*
Simon & Schuster, 1997 pap., ISBN 0-689-80777-5. 202p.
- Grades 10–12

Steve York is a high school senior with a very interesting story. He's a National Merit Finalist who's drugged out and flunking out of school. How can this be? With the help of his guidance counselor, who offers to help him graduate with the required English credits if he writes a paper about his life, Steve begins to chronicle what happened between his sophomore year in Texas and his senior year in California. In the process Steve begins to learn about himself and to grow in positive ways. An excellent young adult novel.

97   Trueman, Terry. *Stuck in Neutral.*
    HarperTempest, 2000 pap., ISBN 978-0-06-447213-5. 114p.
    ▪ **Grades 8–11**

Shawn McDaniel is a fourteen-year-old boy who has spent his entire life confined to a wheelchair. Because of cerebral palsy, he is unable to voluntarily move any muscles in his body. The book chronicles his view of the world and the struggles he endures while seeing and hearing but not moving. Shawn begins to suspect that his father may be trying to kill him to end his "suffering." This is a *very* powerful young adult novel that will have readers flipping the pages to find out what happens to Shawn.

98   Van Draanen, Wendelin. *Flipped.*
    Knopf, 2001, ISBN 978-0-375-81174-6. 212p. ▪ **Grades 6–8**

Eighth-grader Bryce Loski has been trying to avoid his neighbor Juli since she moved to the neighborhood in the second grade. But during his eighth-grade year things start to change — for both of them. The two characters tell the story in alternating chapters, and the reader learns how their relationship "flips." Bryce begins to fall for Juli, and Juli realizes that maybe Bryce isn't everything she thought he was.

Adventure Stories

Adventure has long been an appealing genre for boys. Since the days of *Robinson Crusoe* and *Treasure Island*, adventure books have been written almost exclusively with boys in mind. As John Rowe Townsend notes in *Written for Children*, "For boys there was the life of action on land and at sea: the world of the 'boys' adventure story."

The titles in this section all feature strong adventure themes. Many are in series. These books will expose boys to different styles of adventure and prompt them to seek out other books in the genre.

99   Balliett, Blue. *Chasing Vermeer.*
    Scholastic, 2004, ISBN 978-0-439-37294-7. 272p.
    ▪ **Grades 5–7**

Calder and Petra, sixth-graders in the same class, barely know each other. When they discover they have many similar interests, including a love of art, they become determined to solve the mystery of a missing Vermeer painting. Using clues given throughout the book, they're able to piece together the complex puzzle and solve the mystery before the painting is destroyed. The sequel is *The Wright 3* (see below).

100   Balliett, Blue. *The Wright 3.*

Scholastic, 2006, ISBN 978-0-439-69367-7. 318p.
- Grades 5–7

Calder and Petra are back, and Calder's best friend Tommy joins them in this new mystery involving the possible destruction of architect Frank Lloyd Wright's Robie House. Each of the three brings unique talents to solving the mystery, and their teacher's help and encouragement adds to the mix. This will be another page-turner for fans of the first book, *Chasing Vermeer*.

101   deGuzman, Michael. *The Bamboozlers.*

Farrar, Straus & Giroux, 2005, ISBN 978-0-374-30512-3. 176p. ■ Grades 4–6

Albert Rosegarden is a twelve-year-old boy who is tired of traveling from small town to small town with his single mother. When his grandfather comes to town, he takes Albert to Seattle, and introduces him to many of his old friends and colleagues. Soon they're deeply involved in a scheme to con major money from an old enemy of Albert's grandfather. Albert learns a lot about his family and himself during the adventure. DeGuzman has also written *Beekman's Big Deal* (see entry 63).

102   Hiaasen, Carl. *Flush.*

Knopf Books for Young Readers, 2005, ISBN 978-0-375-82182-0. 272p. ■ Grades 5–7

Hiaasen is at it again with another fun-filled environmental story. This time it involves Noah and his sister Abby, who are caught off-guard when their father is arrested for sinking a casino boat that he believes is dumping raw sewage. The siblings try to prove that their father is correct and this effort leads them to a cast of crazy characters. Fans of *Hoot* will enjoy Hiaasen's second title for younger readers.

103   Hobbs, Will. *Crossing the Wire.*
HarperCollins, 2006, ISBN 978-0-06-074138-9. 192p.
- **Grades 5–8**

Fifteen-year-old Victor and his family are struggling to survive in their Mexican village. Victor's best friend, Rico, tells him he has raised enough money to hire a "coyote" to help him cross the U.S. border, and he invites Victor to join him. Initially Victor turns him down, but when his family's struggles worsen, he decides it's time for him to make the crossing. Readers will pull for Victor as he runs from thieves and the police, and finds both friends and enemies along the way. This well-told story tackles the current issue of illegal immigration.

104   Hobbs, Will. *Far North.*
HarperCollins, 1996, ISBN 978-0-688-14192-9. 240p.
- **Grades 5–8**

Gabe is fifteen years old and attending a boarding school in the Northwest Territories of Canada so he can be closer to his father, an oil field worker. When he gets on a single-engine plane to visit his father, he is joined by his roommate, who has become so depressed that he wants to drop out of school, and his roommate's elderly uncle. The trip is more than they bargained for: First the plane crashes on the river, then winter sets in and the trio must fight to stay alive. This survival novel will have readers riveted (and freezing cold, no matter what the temperature is). Comparing this book to *Hatchet* (see entry 116) and *Brian's Winter* (entry 115) will lead to great discussions.

105   Hobbs, Will. *Leaving Protection.*
HarperCollins, 2004, ISBN 978-0-688-17475-0. 192p.
- **Grades 6–9**

Robbie Daniels is excited because he's finally sixteen, old enough to work on a fishing boat during Alaska's summer salmon season. It's hard work, but can bring in great money for college. Robbie struggles to find a boat willing to hire him but finally finds success with a captain named Tor. Robbie learns that it will be just the two of them on the boat, meaning more work for both of them. When Robbie finds out that the captain is fishing for more than salmon — and digging up old Russian plaques — he becomes concerned about the true nature of Tor's character. What will Tor do when he learns Robbie has discovered his secret? Readers will be desperate to know what happens to Robbie in this action-packed adventure. Hobbs adds an author's note that talks about his own experiences on a boat during the summer salmon season.

106   Hobbs, Will. *River Thunder.*
Delacorte, 1997, ISBN 978-0-385-32316-1. 208p.
- Grades 6–9

All the characters from *Downriver* (1991) are back in this sequel. This time they are brought together believing that their former guide, Al, wants them to be camp counselors. When the truth is discovered — that troublesome Troy has bankrolled the entire operation to get the group back together — they must decide if they want to try rafting through the Grand Canyon together. They agree to make the trip, but when Troy's true motives are discovered and the river water level reaches a record high, the group finds itself in serious danger. This and *Downriver* are excellent adventure stories based on the author's many rafting trips through the Grand Canyon.

107   Hobbs, Will. *Wild Man Island.*
HarperCollins, 2002, ISBN 978-0-688-17473-6. 192p.
- Grades 5–8

Fourteen-year-old Andy, on a sea-kayaking trip in Alaska, decides to make a quick visit to the area where his father died accidentally years earlier. A storm blows him off course and he ends up stranded on a deserted island. On the island he must struggle to find food and shelter while dealing with wild animals and a strange man whom he calls "wild man." Hobbs takes the reader on a great adventure that includes some episodes based on actual events in his life.

108   Korman, Gordon. *Chasing the Falconers.*
Apple, 2005 pap., ISBN 0-439-65137-9. 160p. **Series: On the Run.** - Grades 4–6

This six-book series chronicles the adventures of Aiden and Meg after their parents are convicted of espionage. The thirteen-year-old brother and eleven-year-old sister are kept at a juvenile delinquent facility for their own safety. They break out, hoping to gather evidence to prove that their parents aren't spies. When they become fugitives, they find that it's difficult to solve a mystery while trying to stay one step ahead of the FBI and their newly discovered enemies. The books in this fast-paced adventure series average 160 pages. The other five books are *The Fugitive Factor*, *Now You See Them, Now You Don't*, *Stowaway Solution*, *Public Enemies*, and *Hunting the Hunter*. Kidnapped is a sequel series.

109   Korman, Gordon. *The Contest.*
Scholastic, 2002 pap., ISBN 0-439-40139-9. 96p. **Series: Everest.** ▪ **Grades 4–6**

Four kids are chosen for the ultimate honor: to be the youngest person ever to climb Mount Everest. If the competition to be one of the final four is difficult, imagine the challenges once the climbing begins. This series takes the reader through the contest and the climb to the summit of Everest. The other two books in the series are *The Climb* and *The Summit*.

110   Korman, Gordon. *The Discovery.*
Scholastic, 2003 pap., ISBN 0-439-50722-7. 144p. **Series: Dive.** ▪ **Grades 4–6**

Four teens are chosen from a pool of applicants to go on a diving expedition. They seem to have little in common but come to understand why they were chosen. They discover that the adults on the expedition team are after buried treasure. When the secret is out, the danger level rises. The other books in this adventure trilogy are *The Deep* and *The Danger*.

111   Korman, Gordon. *Kidnapped: The Abduction.*
Apple, 2006 pap., ISBN 0-439-84779-6. 160p. **Series: Kidnapped.** ▪ **Grades 4–6**

This good series follows the six books in On the Run (see entry 108). After surviving as fugitives and proving that their parents weren't spies, Aiden and his sister Meg try to adjust to normal life. But on the way home from school one day Meg is kidnapped and the adventure starts up all over again. This time Meg must try to survive — and escape — on her own. In the meantime, Aiden is trying to find her with the help of a few friends. Aiden and Meg learn their lives may never again be the same, and that there are not many people they can trust. The other books in the series, averaging 160 pages, are *The Search* and *The Rescue*.

112   Korman, Gordon. *Shipwreck*.
Scholastic, 2001 pap., ISBN 0-439-16456-7. 129p. **Series: Island.** ▪ Grades 4–6

Six troubled teens are the reluctant crew on a character-building outing on a sailboat. When the boat sinks in a storm, the teens are shipwrecked. Now they must pull together to survive in this thrilling trilogy. The other books are *Survival* and *Escape*.

113   Paulsen, Gary. *Brian's Hunt*.
Wendy Lamb Books, 2003, ISBN 978-0-385-74647-2. 112p. **Series: Hatchet.** ▪ Grades 5–7

In the final book in the series that began with *Hatchet*, Brian is sixteen and back living in the wild. He finds a badly injured dog, and when taking it to the Cree man he met in *Brian's Return*, he discovers that the man and his wife have been killed and partially eaten by a bear. This begins another adventure for Brian as he sets out to hunt the bear. For more information about Paulsen's inspiration for the Hatchet series, readers can check out *Guts: The True Stories Behind Hatchet and the Brian Books* (see entry 375).

114   Paulsen, Gary. *Brian's Return*.
Delacorte, 1999, ISBN 978-0-385-32500-4. 128p. **Series: Hatchet.** ▪ Grades 5–7

In this sequel to *Brian's Winter*, the reader finds Brian struggling to fit into modern society after surviving in the wilderness for so long. He decides to visit the site of his rescue because he finds he longs for nature. But Brian is once again challenged by nature and the life he has come to love. Readers will enjoy taking another trip with Brian.

115   Paulsen, Gary. *Brian's Winter.*
Delacorte, 1996, ISBN 978-0-385-32198-3. 144p. **Series:
Hatchet.** ▪ **Grades 5–7**

In this book Paulsen writes about what would have happened to
Brian Robeson if he hadn't been rescued after the plane crash he
survived in *Hatchet*. He endures his first winter alone after the
crash, facing cold, hunger, and danger. The other two books in the
Brian series are *Brian's Return* and *Brian's Hunt* (see above).

116   Paulsen, Gary. *Hatchet.*
Atheneum, 2000, ISBN 978-1-4287-2239-2. 208p. **Series:
Hatchet.** ▪ **Grades 4–6**
✪ **Newbery Honor Book**

Brian is on a small plane on the way to visit his father. When the
pilot has a heart attack and dies, Brian, who is thirteen years old and
the only passenger, must land the plane. Stranded way off course, he
fights to survive for more than a month in the wild. Readers will root
for Brian as he uses his wits and the only tool he has — a hatchet —
to keep himself alive.

117   Philbrick, Rodman. *The Young Man and the Sea.*
Blue Sky Press, 2004, ISBN 978-0-439-36829-2. 192p.
▪ **Grades 5–8**

Skiff's mother has died and his father is drowning his sorrows in
alcohol. Twelve-year-old Skiff repairs his father's neglected fishing
boat with the help of some generous neighbors and one day sets off
on a fishing trip for a bluefin. But he hadn't planned on actually
hooking a great tuna. Now he must land the huge fish and bring him
back to shore with only limited supplies. Great comparisons can be
made between this book and Hemingway's *The Old Man and the
Sea*.

118   Smelcer, John. *The Trap.*
Holt, 2006, ISBN 0-8050-7939-4. 170p. ▪ **Grades 5–7**

Seventeen-year-old Johnny Least-Weasel worries about his grandfather when the old man fails to return from checking his trap line.
The weather turns colder and Johnny knows he must go find his
grandfather before it's too late. Alternating chapters allow the reader

to find out what is happening to the grandfather in one chapter and to Johnny in the next. Readers will root for both Johnny and his grandfather as the suspenseful adventure unfolds.

119   Smith, Roland. *Jack's Run.*
Hyperion, 2005, ISBN 978-0-7868-5592-6. 246p.
- Grades 6 and up

In this sequel to *Zach's Lie* (2001), Jack Osborne is still on the run. His father is about to testify against a drug czar. Jack's whole family is under government protection. Jack is sent to live with his sister in Los Angeles and his sister's appearance on a TV game show leads to their kidnapping. After they are taken to South America, the story is told in alternating chapters that give both Jack's and his sister's side of the story.

120   Smith, Roland. *Peak.*
Harcourt, 2007, ISBN 978-0-15-202417-8. 256p. ■ Grades 6 and up

Fourteen-year-old Peak loves to climb. He loves it so much that he gets in trouble for climbing skyscrapers in his hometown of New York City. To avoid jail time, he sets off to visit his father in Thailand and discovers that his father has plans for him to be the youngest person ever to climb Mount Everest. As Peak gets closer to the summit he learns more about himself and must make a very difficult decision. A great adventure for fans of action-packed stories.

121   Snicket, Lemony. *The Bad Beginning.*
HarperCollins, 1999, ISBN 978-0-06-440766-3. 163p. Series: Series of Unfortunate Events. ■ Grades 4–6

In the first book of this series, readers meet the Baudelaire children, who lose their parents and home in a fire. When they are sent to live with their new guardian, Count Olaf, their troubles really start. The count has only one thing on his mind: getting his hands on the Baudelaire fortune. The three siblings work to outsmart Count Olaf and to stay together. Readers will be eager to read the entire thirteen-book series, full of adventure and humor. Lemony Snicket does a great job of presenting new vocabulary in a fun and nonthreatening way. There are twelve other books in the series: *The Reptile Room,*

The Wide Window, The Miserable Mill, The Austere Academy, The Ersatz Elevator, The Vile Village, The Hostile Hospital, The Carnivorous Carnival, The Slippery Slope, The Grim Grotto, The Penultimate Peril, and *The End.*

Sports Stories

Boys and sports go hand in hand. The sports in the books included here range from conventional team sports (such as football, baseball, and basketball) to less-conventional pursuits (such as bowling, auto racing, and fishing).

Probably the best-known author of sports-themed books for children is Matt Christopher. This section goes beyond Christopher's work to include titles by many other authors. It includes stories that are funny, suspenseful, and intense, and that focus on much more than "the big game." It's my hope that this chapter will serve as an introduction to a variety of authors and titles, encouraging boys to hunt down even more sports books in the library on their own.

Picture Books

122   Shannon, David. *How Georgie Radbourn Saved Baseball.*

Scholastic, 1994 pap., ISBN 978-0-590-47411-5. 32p.
- **Grades 3–4**

Georgie Radbourn was born into a town that has only one season: winter. Georgie has a unique talent — speaking only in baseball slang terms. His parents try hard to hide this "gift." But mean Boss Swaggert hears of it, and trouble is in store for Georgie. Georgie challenges the bigger and stronger Boss to a baseball competition. The results change the town forever and even bring back the four seasons. Beautiful illustrations by Shannon accompany the text.

Novels

123   Avi. *The Mayor of Central Park.*

Ill. by Brian Floca. HarperCollins, 2003, ISBN 978-0-06-000682-2. 208p. ▪ **Grades 3–5**

Oscar Westerwit is a squirrel living in Central Park in 1900. He considers himself mayor of the park and manager of the Green Sox, the squirrel baseball team. But trouble is brewing in Central Park as rats, led by mean Big Daddy Duds, start to take over. There's only one way to resolve this: a baseball game. Readers will root for the squirrels throughout this fun novel.

124   Bloor, Edward. *Tangerine.*

Harcourt, 1997, ISBN 978-0-15-201246-5. 303p.
▪ **Grades 6–8**

Paul Fisher starts seventh grade in Florida after his family moves there from Texas. Paul, who was partially blinded in a childhood incident, is determined to make friends, succeed in school, and play on the school soccer team. Paul's life is challenged by what goes on at home. His older brother Erik is idolized because of his football abilities. Paul starts to meet his goals and discovers some of Erik's secrets that date back to Paul's accident. A good coming-of-age and underdog story.

125   Coy, John. *Strong to the Hoop.*

Ill. by Leslie Jean-Bart. Lee & Low, 1999, ISBN 978-1-880000-80-9. 32p. ▪ **Grades 3–5**

James is ten years old and finally gets the chance to play in a basketball game with his older brother's friends. Fans of basketball will enjoy the pace of the game, and how James copes with playing with bigger and older boys.

126 Coy, John, Antonio Reonegro, and Tom Lynch. *Around the World.*

Lee & Low, 2005, ISBN 978-1-58430-244-5. 32p.
- Grades 3–5

This picture book takes the reader through nine different basketball games around the globe. Beginning in New York City the book jumps to games in Australia, China, Turkey, and other locations before returning to New York City. Boys will enjoy the game of basketball no matter where it is being played.

127 DeFelice, Cynthia. *The Missing Manatee.*

Farrar, Straus & Giroux, 2005, ISBN 0-374-31257-5. 181p.
- Grades 4–6

Skeet Waters is an eleven-year-old boy who loves fishing. As he struggles with his parents' divorce he gets to fish with an older friend for the big fish, a lifelong dream of Skeet's. But after viewing a manatee that has been murdered Skeet learns that not everyone and everything is as it seems. Skeet grows up a little and learns how to fish, accept others, and find his place in the world.

128 Feinstein, John. *Cover-Up: Mystery at the Super Bowl.*

Knopf, 2007, ISBN 978-0-375-84247-4. 304p. - Grades 6–9

Stevie Thomas and Susan Carol are fourteen-year-old sports fans and aspiring journalists. In this third book about them, they stumble upon a mystery at the Super Bowl, and their lives may be in danger if they publish the story. This is a fast-paced novel that will have boys excited to find out what happens next. The two other books with these detective teens are *Vanishing Act: Mystery at the U.S. Open* (2006) and *Last Shot: A Final Four Mystery* (2006), set at the NCAA basketball tournament.

129 Glenn, Mel. *Jump Ball! A Basketball Season in Poems.*

Dutton, 1997, ISBN 978-0-525-67554-9. 160p.
- Grades 8–11

This free-verse novel tells of the Tower High School championship basketball season. The reader learns about the lives of the players, the culture of the high school, and what the team faces throughout the season. A good young adult poetic novel.

130   Gorman, Carol, and Ron Findley. *Stumptown Kid.*

Peachtree, 2005, ISBN 1-56145-337-4. 224p. ▪ **Grades 4–6**

Charlie Nebraska is almost twelve years old and absolutely *loves* baseball. When he fails to make the town team, a stranger named Luther begins to coach him and a few of his friends. The kids think nothing of the fact that Luther's an African American. However, in this 1950s small town this brings out racial issues, and Charlie learns a lot about baseball, life, friendship, and discrimination. Try pairing this book with *Satchel Paige* (entry 314) and *Satch and Me* (entry 135).

131   Green, Tim. *Football Genius.*

HarperCollins, 2007, ISBN 978-0-06-112270-5. 256p.
▪ **Grades 5–7**

Twelve-year-old Troy White is a good football player, but he can't show it because he's stuck behind the coach's son on the team. He also has the ability to accurately predict what will happen next on the field. When his mother gets a job with his favorite professional team, the Atlanta Falcons, he sees a chance to share his gift with the team. But no one will listen to him until he convinces the star linebacker, Seth Halloway, of his talent. Then the two help the Falcons gain a "secret edge."

132   Gutman, Dan. *Casey Back at Bat.*

Ill. by Steve Johnson and Lou Fancher. HarperCollins, 2007, ISBN 0-06-056025-8. 32p. ▪ **Grades 3–4**

In this "sequel" to the poem "Casey at the Bat," Casey gets a second chance. This time he crushes a home run, and readers follow its path as it leaves the stadium, country, galaxy, even going back in time. Readers will enjoy the humorous path the ball takes.

133   Gutman, Dan. *The Million Dollar Shot.*

Hyperion, 2006 pap., ISBN 978-1-4231-0084-3. 128p.
▪ **Grades 4–6**

When Eddie Ball's mother and his neighbor Annie's father both lose their jobs at Finkle Foods, things don't look good. Eddie and Annie decide to enter a poetry contest that allows the winner the chance to shoot a free throw for a million dollars. When Eddie's poem is chosen, the pressure is on — from himself, his friends, and even Mr. Finkle, who is offering the huge prize.

134   Gutman, Dan. *The Million Dollar Strike.*
Hyperion, 2004, ISBN 978-0-7868-1880-8. 192p.
- Grades 4–6

Ouchie and Squishy love to bowl at the Bowl-a-Rama run by eccentric Mr. Zamboni. So when the city council condemns the bowling alley, Ouchie and Squishy vow to save it. Enlisting the help of Mr. Zamboni (who thinks the world will end soon anyway), they stumble upon a bigger mystery. The boys learn who wants the bowling alley closed and how far they're willing to go. Other books in the series are *The Million Dollar Shot* (see above), *The Million Dollar Goal*, *The Million Dollar Kick*, and *The Million Dollar Putt*.

135   Gutman, Dan. *Satch and Me.*
Amistad, 2006, ISBN 978-0-06-059491-6. 192p. **Series: Baseball Card Adventures.** - Grades 4–6

Thirteen-year-old Joe Stosh has the unique talent of traveling through time by holding a baseball card. In this story he wonders who threw the fastest pitch ever. The adventure begins when his coach tells him it was Satchel Paige. Joe decides to take his coach back in time with him, and when they meet Paige they learn more about his explosive personality and the hardships he endured. Other books in the series are *Babe and Me*, *Mickey and Me*, *Jackie and Me*, *Shoeless Joe and Me*, *Honus and Me*, and *Abner and Me*.

136   Jennings, Patrick. *Out Standing in My Field.*
Scholastic, 2005, ISBN 978-0-439-46581-6. 165p.
- Grades 4–6

Ty Cutter loves playing baseball, but he's horrible at it. What makes it worse is that he's forced to play every inning of every game because his father is the team coach. This leads to taunting and ridicule from his teammates. The only person on the team who will talk to him is his sister Daisy, the scorekeeper. During one game, the brother and sister discuss their family, themselves, and baseball, helping Ty decide what he should do about his future as a ballplayer.

137   Lewin, Ted. *At Gleason's Gym.*
Roaring Brook Press, 2007, ISBN 978-1-59643-231-4. 40p.
- Grades 3–4

Gleason's Gym in Brooklyn, New York, is a famous boxing gym that has seen the likes of Muhammad Ali and others train there. Now Sugar Boy Younan, a nine-year-old Silver Gloves champion is training there. Readers meet the different people who work and train at the gym as well as learning more about the world of boxing.

138   Lipsythe, Robert. *Raiders Night.*
HarperTeen, 2006, ISBN 978-0-06-059946-1. 240p.
- Grades 9–11

Matt Rydek is a senior in high school and co-captain of the football team. Drugs, alcohol, and sex are part of football stardom in his town. When a hazing incident goes bad at football camp the chemistry of the team changes dramatically, and Matt must decide whether to remain silent to protect his teammates — or to tell the truth and become an outcast. This is a disturbing and violent novel for older readers.

139   Lipsythe, Robert. *Yellow Flag.*
HarperTeen, 2007, ISBN 978-0-06-055707-2. 240p.
- Grades 9–11

Kyle's family is one of the most famous in car racing. His older brother Kris followed in his father's footsteps while Kyle pursued music. When Kris has a bad accident and can't race, Kyle is asked to step in. Deciding between helping his family and living his dream is tough. When Kyle shows promise as a driver and receives sponsorship offers, the decision becomes even more difficult. Readers will be racing to the end of this fast-paced story.

140   Lupica, Mike. *Summer Ball.*
Philomel, 2007, ISBN 978-0-399-24487-2. 244p.
- Grades 6–8

Thirteen-year-old Danny Walker loves basketball more than anything. The summer before ninth grade he and his friends go to a big basketball camp and Danny's love of the game is put to the test. He learns that being a smaller player means he needs to adjust his game and play big. Danny learns about his favorite sport, life, and friendship. This is a conventional sports story in which the main character succeeds in the end. Other sports books by Lupica include *Travel Team* (2004) and *Heat* (2006).

141   Miller, William. *Night Golf.*

Ill. by Cedric Lucas. Lee & Low, 1999, ISBN 978-1-880000-79-3. 32p. ▪ **Grades 3–4**

James is a young African American boy growing up in the 1950s. When he discovers an abandoned golf club in the trash he falls in love with the sport. Soon he takes on a job as a caddy at the town's only golf course, an all-white course. When he's befriended by an older caddy he learns about night golf, when African Americans can practice and enjoy the sport they love so much. Later James must show how good he really is at the game.

142   Parker, Robert B. *Edenville Owls.*

Philomel, 2007, ISBN 0-399-24656-8. 224p. ▪ **Grades 6–8**

Fourteen-year-old Bobby senses something is just not right at his school. When he sees and learns things about his new English teacher he enlists the help of his small-school, coachless basketball team. The team comes together both on and off the court to grow as a group and help others at the same time. A good mix of mystery and sports.

143   Ritter, John H. *Under the Baseball Moon.*

Philomel, 2006, ISBN 0-399-23623-6. 283p. ▪ **Grades 8–11**

Soon-to-be tenth-grader Andy Ramos loves to play his trumpet. He and his buddies form a band called FuChar Skool, and Andy hopes his music will take him far. But when he makes a deal with the devil, meets a long-lost friend, and falls in love, his summer changes drastically. Readers will be spellbound as they learn what happens to Andy and the deal he made. A good combination of sports and music.

144 Spinelli, Jerry. *Crash.*

Knopf, 1996, ISBN 978-0-679-87957-2. 176p. ▪ **Grades 5–7**

Crash Coogan is a stereotypical jock. He loves pounding guys on the football field. But when his grandfather suffers a stroke and moves in with Crash and his family, things begin to change. He starts to see his neighbor Penn, whom Crash has bullied for years, in a different light. A friendship grows and Crash learns there is more to life than football.

145 Tavares, Matt. *Mudball.*

Candlewick, 2005, ISBN 978-0-7636-2387-6. 32p.
▪ **Grades 3–4**

In 1903 Andy Oyler is the shortest player in the major leagues. In a rainsoaked game the umpire allows Andy to bat, thinking he will make the final out and end the game. When Andy connects with the ball it gets stuck in the mud in the infield and Andy's home run begins. Readers will enjoy the humor of the story and illustrations about underdog Andy. Other books by Matt Tavares include *Zachary's Ball* (2000) and *Oliver's Game* (2004).

146 Valponi, Paul. *Rucker Park Setup.*

Viking, 2007, ISBN 978-0-670-06130-3. 149p.
▪ **Grades 8–11**

Teenager Mackey and his best friend J.R. dreamed of playing together in a basketball tournament. But then J.R. is stabbed to death on the very court where the tournament is to take place. Mackey must face the truth of his involvement in what happened to J.R. while sorting through the deceit that surrounds his friend's death. He goes on to play in the tournament with J.R.'s dad as the referee. Readers will be pulling for Mackey to do the right thing in this gripping book.

147 Wallace, Rich. *Winning Season: Curveball.*

Viking, 2007, ISBN 978-0-670-06119-8. 112p. **Series: Winning Season.** ▪ **Grades 3–5**

Eddie Ventura plays on the Hudson City Hornets baseball team and also writes about it for the school newspaper — under a different name. His accounts cause a stir among his teammates. Readers who love baseball will enjoy his detailed accounts of the games. Additional books in the series are *Southpaw*, *Dunk Under Pressure*, *Takedown*, and *Second String Center*.

148   Weaver, Will. *Farm Team.*
HarperTeen, 1995 pap., ISBN 978-0-06-447118-3. 288p.
- Grades 8–10

Billy Baggs, a shy fourteen-year-old, sees his chance to play summer league baseball vanish when his father is sentenced to three months in jail. His mother tries to help out and assembles a ragtag team using other farm workers, neighbors, and even the family dog. The "farm team" turns out to be pretty good, and challenges the city team to a game. This is a classic underdog story that is especially well written. Billy Baggs can also be found in Weaver's *Striking Out* (1993).

Sources
Kiefer, B., Hickman, J., & Hepler S. (2006). *Charlotte Huck's Children's Literature*. McGraw-Hill.

Townsend, John R. (2006). *Written for Children*. Scarecrow.

Chapter 4

Fantasy

There has always been a high demand for fantasy books among boy readers. Charlotte S. Huck has written: "if we always give children stories of 'what is,' stories that only mirror the living of today, then we have not helped them to imagine 'what might have been,' or 'what might be'" (Kiefer, Hepler, Hickman, 2006). From high fantasy to science fiction, stories about different worlds appeal to readers of all ages. Boys enjoy finding themselves in new lands or among new people.

The titles found in this section include books with aliens, magic, time travel, and other fantastic elements that will fascinate boys. This chapter is divided into two sections: General Fantasy (subdivided into Picture Books and Novels) and Animal Fantasy.

General Fantasy
Picture Books

149 **Schlitz, Laura Amy. *The Bearskinner: A Tale of the Brother's Grimm.***
Ill. by Max Grafe. Candlewick, 2007, ISBN 978-0-7636-2730-0. 40p. ▪ Grades 4–6

A man makes a deal with the devil — he can be rich as long as he wears for seven straight years the skin of a bear he just killed. Readers will be intrigued by the deal and what the man does, as well as by the amazing illustrations that accompany the story.

150   Scieszka, Jon. *Baloney (Henry P.)*.
Ill. by Lane Smith. Viking, 2001, ISBN 978-0-670-89248-8. 32p. ▪ Grades 2–5

Henry P. Baloney is late for school one time too many. When his teacher asks him why he's late, Henry P. launches into a story about adventures with aliens, mixing in words from different languages. A glossary is included to help readers learn the unknown words. A very funny story and a wonderful way to learn new words.

151   Van Allsburg, Chris. *Probuditi!*
Houghton Mifflin, 2006, ISBN 978-0-618-75502-8. 32p. ▪ Grades 2–3

Calvin and his buddy Rodney celebrate Calvin's birthday by attending a show by a hypnotist. Enthralled by a hypnotized woman clucking like a chicken, Calvin tries to hypnotize his sister, Trudy, and make her act like a dog. Everything works well, until Calvin and Rodney try to end the spell. With some help from — of all people — Trudy, normality is restored. Van Allsburg's excellent illustrations add to the appeal.

152   Van Allsburg, Chris. *Zathura*.
Houghton Mifflin, 2002, ISBN 978-0-618-25396-8. 32p. ▪ Grades 3–5

In this masterfully created sequel to Caldecott winner *Jumanji* (1981), Danny and Walter Budwing find the Jumanji game. Not impressed with the jungle game board, they dig a bit deeper in the box and find a space game board. This time the game takes them into outer space and to planet Zathura. The boys must figure out a way to get home safely.

153   Wiesner, David. *Flotsam*.
Clarion, 2006, ISBN 978-0-618-19457-5. 40p. ▪ Grades 3–5
✪ Caldecott Medal

An excellent wordless picture book depicting a young boy playing on the beach. When he finds a camera he decides to develop the film still inside. He sees photographs of underwater scenes and of other children who have taken pictures with the camera. The boy decides to continue the cycle. He takes a picture of himself and throws the camera back into the ocean. Readers will create new stories each time they open the cover of this complex wordless book.

154   Wiesner, David. *Sector 7.*

Clarion, 1999, ISBN 978-0-395-74656-1. 48p. ▪ **Grades 3–5**
✪ **Caldecott Honor Book**

Another wordless picture-book adventure by Wiesner. A young boy on a class field trip to the Empire State Building is befriended by a cloud. Together they run off to Sector 7, the dispatch center for clouds. The clouds, unhappy with their boring shapes, enlist the boy's artistic skills to make their shapes more interesting. This creates disharmony at the dispatch center and the boy is escorted back to his class. But the clouds in New York City are now much more interesting to look at. Readers will delight in telling their own stories by following the pictures.

Novels

155   Almond, David. *Skellig.*

Delacorte, 1999, ISBN 978-0-385-32653-7. 192p.
▪ **Grades 4–6**
✪ **Michael L. Printz Award**

Michael and his family have just moved. He is unhappy with his new surroundings and his family's stress over his very ill baby sister. While exploring their new house Michael stumbles upon a mysterious creature in the garage. Unsure if it's an alien, a bird, or a human, Michael can't take his mind off the creature, called Skellig. Soon he befriends a neighbor, Mina, and enlists her to help him nurse Skellig back to health and find out what Skellig is. Their lives interconnect with Skellig's and soon everyone's life is changing. This book would pair well with Avi's *The Christmas Rat* (see entry 157).

156   Anderson, M. T. *Feed.*
Candlewick, 2002, ISBN 978-0-7636-1726-4. 240p.
■ **Grades 8–11**

In this futuristic novel, the main character, Titus, is a typical teenager who has the Internet hooked up to his brain. Like everyone else. It's called the "feed," and it constantly bombards people with information and advertising. When Titus and his friends go to the moon for spring break it's the usual teen trip — until Titus meets Violet. Violet is home-schooled and has only an antiquated version of the feed. She tries to point out to Titus and his friends that they're really being brainwashed. Titus falls hard for Violet and learns a lot about her, about himself, and most importantly, about the influence the feed is having on everyone's lives.

157   Avi. *The Christmas Rat.*
Atheneum, 2000, ISBN 978-0-689-83842-2. 144p.
■ **Grades 4–6**

Eric is bored during the first week of his Christmas vacation and welcomes the diversion when an exterminator comes to spray his apartment building for rats. When he meets the exterminator, who goes by the name of Anjela Gabriela, Eric wonders about this mysterious person. Soon Eric finds himself trying to protect the hunted rat and to determine who and what Anjela Gabriela truly is. A well-told mystery that will leave readers wondering who Eric really met during his Christmas break. This book would pair well with David Almond's *Skellig* (see above).

158   Avi. *Seer of Shadows.*
HarperCollins, 2008, ISBN 978-0-06-000016-5. 208p.
■ **Grades 4–7**

It's New York City in 1872 and young Horace Carpetine is a photographer's apprentice. The position is not that interesting until Horace's master takes on the job of photographing a ghost. The photographer believes he can trick his client by doctoring photos. Horace is uncomfortable with this trickery, and his troubles are compounded when he discovers he has a gift for "freeing" actual ghosts by photographing them. A ghost Horace frees seeks revenge on those who killed her, and Horace must find a way to "rebind" this vengeful ghost before other lives are lost, including his own.

159 **Barron, T. A. *The Lost Years of Merlin.***
Ace, 1999 pap., ISBN 978-0-441-00668-7. 304p. **Series: The Lost Years of Merlin.** ▪ **Grades 5–7**

This is the first of five books chronicling the childhood and growth of the great magician Merlin. When he finds himself washed up on a foreign shore, his memory erased, Merlin is taken in by a woman who claims to be his mother. He sets out on his own to discover his origins, and eventually finds himself in the place where he was born among people now making great demands of him. The sequels are *The Seven Songs of Merlin, The Fires of Merlin, The Mirror of Merlin,* and *The Wings of Merlin.*

160 **Colfer, Eoin. *Artemis Fowl.***
Miramax, 2001, ISBN 978-0-7868-0801-4. 288p. **Series: Artemis Fowl.** ▪ **Grades 5–7**

Twelve-year-old Artemis Fowl comes from a formerly famous crime family. He decides to restore its legendary status by committing the ultimate crime: stealing a pot of gold from the "fairy folk." He decides that the best method is to kidnap a fairy and wait for the ransom. Unfortunately for Artemis, he kidnaps a member of the LEPrecon (Lower Elements Police Reconnaissance Unit), who will stop at nothing to get their colleague back. High-tech gadgets and wild adventure reign in this first book of the series. Readers will enjoy the conflict between modern times and the fantasy world. Other books in the series are *Artemis Fowl: The Arctic Incident, Artemis Fowl: The Eternity Code, Artemis Fowl: The Opal Deception,* and *Artemis Fowl: The Lost Colony.*

161 **Collins, Suzanne. *Gregor the Overlander.***
Scholastic, 2003, ISBN 978-0-439-43536-9. 320p. **Series: Underland Chronicles.** ▪ **Grades 4–7**

Young Gregor and his baby sister fall into an underground world filled with oversized bats, cockroaches, and vicious rats. Gregor just wants to find the way home, even when the creatures present him with the possibility that he's their overlord. Not until the animals tell him that his father — who has been missing for years — is being held captive by the rats does Gregor become their hero. This action-filled novel will appeal to fantasy fans. This, the first book in the Underland Chronicles, is followed by *Gregor and the Prophecy of the Bane*, *Gregor and the Curse of the Warmbloods*, *Gregor and the Marks of the Secret*, and *Gregor and the Code of the Claw*.

162   Coville, Bruce. *My Teacher Is an Alien.*
        Simon & Schuster, 1989 pap., ISBN 978-06-71737-29-0.
        123p. Series: My Teacher Is an Alien. ▪ Grades 4–6

Susan and Peter suspect their substitute teacher is an alien. But who would believe that? When they follow their teacher home one day and see him remove his face, they know they have to do something! Then the two hear the plans he has for the rest of their sixth-grade class. Can they save the day and their classmates? Readers will enjoy the idea of a teacher from outer space. Other books in the series are *My Teacher Fried My Brains*, *My Teacher Glows in the Dark*, and *My Teacher Flunked the Planet*.

163   Creech, Sharon. *The Castle Corona.*
        Ill. by David Diaz. Joanna Cotler Books, 2007, ISBN 978-0-06-084621-3. 320p. ▪ Grades 4–6

In a castle in Italy lives a very unhappy royal family. Two of their subjects are a peasant girl and her younger brother, poor orphans. When the sister and brother find a royal purse, a mystery ensues. Soon the lives of the peasant orphans become entwined with those of the royal family, and everyone's lot improves. This entertaining high-fantasy tale with many twists and turns represents a new genre for author Sharon Creech.

164   Delaney, Joseph. *Attack of the Fiend.*
        Ill. by Patrick Arrasmith. Greenwillow, 2008, ISBN 978-0-06-089127-5. 560p. Series: The Last Apprentice. ▪ Grades 5–7

The latest in the Last Apprentice series has Tom and the Spook off to Pendle, the witch capital of the county. When Tom finds that some valuable trunks have been stolen from him and that his family has been kidnapped, the stakes are raised. The trunks have great power, and if they fall into the wrong hands, the world will know a great evil. Tom and the Spook must save the county and Tom faces the greatest danger yet.

165   Delaney, Joseph. *Curse of the Bane.*
Greenwillow, 2005, ISBN 978-0-06-076621-4. 455p. **Series: The Last Apprentice.** ■ **Grades 5–7**

The further adventures of Tom Ward, an apprentice for the Spook. When the Spook announces that they must complete some "unfinished business," Tom learns more about this master who continues to confuse him. While trying to figure out who his friends are and who can help him, Tom comes face-to-face with the curse of the Bane. Fighting the Bane is the only way to save both his master and his friend Alice. Readers will be turning the pages to see if Tom can save himself and the others.

166   Delaney, Joseph. *Night of the Soul Stealer.*
Greenwillow, 2007, ISBN 978-0-06-076624-5. 512p. **Series: The Last Apprentice.** ■ **Grades 5–7**

Tom's master decides it's time for the two of them to travel to his winter home. Here, Tom learns that the Spook is married — to a witch! The witch is one of the worst ones ever, and must be heavily sedated in order to keep her from killing others for their blood. Tom is also haunted by a local boy who was a failed apprentice for the Spook. These two evils combine to become Tom's greatest challenge ever as the Spook's apprentice. This is a darker installment in the series.

167   Delaney, Joseph. *Revenge of the Witch.*
Ill. by Patrick Arrasmith. Greenwillow, 2005, ISBN 978-0-06-076620-7. 344p. **Series: The Last Apprentice.** ■ **Grades 5–7**

Twelve-year-old Thomas Ward is the seventh son of a seventh son. His father has trouble finding an apprenticeship for his last son. His only hope is the great Spook. Tom tries hard to be a good apprentice for this scary man who rids the local villages of evil spirits and magic. When he must decide between keeping a promise and freeing a dangerous witch, Tom learns the hard way about the challenges and pitfalls of his new occupation. This is the first installment in an excellent, darker fantasy series. It is followed by *Curse of the Bane* (see above), *Night of the Soul Stealer* (2007), and *Attack of the Fiend* (see above).

168   Elliott, David. *The Transmogrification of Roscoe Wizzle.*
Candlewick, 2001, ISBN 0-7636-1880-2. 115p. ▪ **Grades 3–5**

What would happen if you ate fast-food hamburgers every day for a month? If you're ten-year-old Roscoe Wizzle, you start turning into a bug. When Roscoe learns he's turning into an insect he stumbles upon a mystery at Gussy's Restaurant. His only hope is to solve the mystery and save not only himself, but also the other children who have been turning into insects. This is an entertaining fantasy for younger readers.

169   Farmer, Nancy. *House of the Scorpion.*
Atheneum, 2002, ISBN 978-0-689-85222-0. 2002p.
▪ **Grades 9–12**
✪ **Newbery Honor Book, Michael L. Printz Honor Book**

This is a very powerful novel addressing many deep issues. Matt is a clone of a powerful drug lord, "El Patrón," in the country of Opium, which lies between the United States and Azatlan (formerly known as Mexico). Matt's existence is a privileged one — he even has his own bodyguard. As Matt starts to learn the truth about El Patrón, he sees what evil lies in the country of Opium. He also learns what El Patrón has in store for him, and he fears for his life. This well-told story will have readers hooked from the beginning.

170   Farmer, Nancy. *The Sea of Trolls.*
Atheneum, 2004, ISBN 0-689-86744-1. 459p. ▪ **Grades 5–8**

Jack is an eleven-year-old whose life isn't very exciting. But when a bard makes Jack his apprentice, things begin to change. Before he can hone his new skills he and his sister are kidnapped. Then Jack casts a spell on the troll queen and is sent on a challenging quest for a remedy. Readers will be entertained and eager to see what happens to Jack in this fantasy adventure set in medieval times. The sequel is *The Land of the Silver Apples.*

171   Funke, Cornelia. *The Thief Lord.*

Scholastic, 2002, ISBN 978-0-439-85271-5. 349p.
- Grades 4–6

Twelve-year-old Prosper and his five-year-old brother Bo are on the run from their aunt, who wants to adopt only Bo. After fleeing Hamburg and arriving in Venice they realize that survival will be difficult. Falling in with a group of orphans, they live in an abandoned movie theater and steal for someone called "the thief lord." The ultimate quest is to steal a wooden wing from a magical carousel with the power to turn adults into children and children into adults. When the thief lord is exposed as a rich child who is stealing from his parents, the orphans must decide if they will stay with him. A private investigator who is hot on the trail of Prosper and Bo adds to the adventure. Cornelia Funke has also written *Inkheart* (Scholastic, 2003) and *Inkspell* (Scholastic, 2005).

172   Hickman, Janet. *Ravine.*

Greenwillow, 2002, ISBN 978-0-688-17952-6. 224p.
- Grades 4–6

Jeremy and his friend Quinn love their toy warriors. They find that the best place to play with them is a ravine near Jeremy's house. When they follow Jeremy's dog, Duchess, into the ravine they enter into a "time slip" that takes them back to the era of their miniature soldiers. Now they enter into a real battle that could cost them their lives. The boys must seek a way back to their modern-day home.

173   Kehret, Peg. *The Ghost's Grave.*

Dutton, 2005, ISBN 0-525-46162-0. 210p. ■ Grades 3–6

Josh is sent to live with an aunt he doesn't know in Oregon. Disappointed that he can't play on the summer baseball team back in Minnesota, he tries to make the best of the situation. But when he meets a ghost, finds a bag of stolen money, and is then hunted by the thief, his summer becomes more exciting than he ever dreamed.

174   Landy, Derek. *Skullduggery Pleasant.*

HarperCollins, 2007, ISBN 978-0-06-123115-5. 400p.
- **Grades 4–7**

When twelve-year-old Stephanie's uncle dies, she inherits his entire estate! It's a rather spooky place to be, especially when you're twelve, and the first time she's there she ends up spending the night alone. Someone wearing a hat and long trench coat saves her from an intruder and she learns she has just met Skullduggery Pleasant, a skeleton who will protect Stephanie from underworld beings who have a grudge against her uncle. Readers will cheer for Stephanie and Skullduggery throughout this action-packed adventure.

175   Lethcoe, Jason. *The Misadventures of Benjamin Bartholomew Piff: You Wish.*

Penguin, 2007, ISBN 978-0-448-44496-3. 215p. **Series: Benjamin Bartholomew Piff.** ■ **Grades 3–5**

Orphaned eleven-year-old Benjamin is living a difficult life. When he gets to make a wish on his birthday, he wisely wishes that all his wishes would come true. It works, but also disrupts the overall balance of wishes. As Benjamin learns more about the wish world, he finds that he's the only one who can restore proper balance. This fun fantasy adventure will prompt boys to rethink their birthday wishes. The other books in this series are *Wishful Thinking* and *Wishing Well*.

176   Mosley, Walter. *47.*

Little, Brown, 2005, ISBN 0-316-11035-3. 232p.
- **Grades 6–8**

A historical fiction tale incorporating a twist of fantasy. A young slave boy called 47 is befriended by the mysterious Tall John, another young slave with amazing magical powers. Tall John teaches 47 about some of his powers and takes him on journeys to other worlds. When a feud breaks out, 47 must choose between saving his fellow slaves and escaping to freedom. This could be paired with *Night John* (Delacorte, 1993) by Gary Paulsen.

177   Nimmo, Jenny. *Midnight for Charlie Bone: The Children of the Red King, Book 1.*
Orchard, 2003, ISBN 978-0-439-47429-0. 416p. **Series: Children of the Red King.** ▪ **Grades 4–6**

When Charlie Bone turns ten he discovers he can hear conversations among people pictured in old photographs. When his grandmother and her sisters find out about this talent, they enroll him at Bloor's Academy, a school for gifted children, to develop Charlie's skills for their own benefit. At school Charlie makes friends, but also discovers he has enemies from age-old rivalries. When Charlie uses the photograph voices to help him find a missing girl, the action really begins. Readers will root for Charlie throughout the adventure. Fans of Harry Potter will enjoy this series. Other books in the series include *Charlie Bone and the Time Twister*, *Charlie Bone and the Invisible Boy*, *Charlie Bone and the Castle of Mirrors*, *Charlie Bone and the Hidden King*, and *Charlie Bone and the Beast*.

178   Oppel, Kenneth. *Airborn.*
HarperCollins, 2004, ISBN 0-06-053180-0. 368p.
▪ **Grades 6–9**
✪ **Michael L. Printz Honor Book**

Imagine a world in which blimps crisscross the oceans. This is the world that Oppel has created in *Airborn*. Matt Cruse works as a cabin boy on one of the airships. He meets a spirited young heiress named Kate and becomes distracted by Kate's secret mission to find the mysterious cloud creatures her uncle saw before he died. When their airship is attacked by pirates, a forced landing provides Matt and Kate the opportunity to come face-to-face with the "cloud cats." But this also puts them into the pirates' den. Their attempt to escape makes for a riveting adventure. The sequel is *Skybreaker* (see below).

179   Oppel, Kenneth. *Skybreaker.*
Eos, 2005, ISBN 978-0-06-053227-7. 369p. ▪ **Grades 9–11**

This action-packed sequel to *Airborn* brings Matt and Kate back together in a quest for gold. Matt is a student at the Airship Academy and trains as a navigator on a cargo ship. When the ship's captain spots a ghost ship rumored to be full of gold, he takes the ship and its crew to dangerous altitudes in pursuit. The entire crew falls victim to altitude sickness and must head home. Only Matt remembers the coordinates of the ghost ship, and the word gets out that he knows. Matt and Kate find the ghost ship and the gold, but not before they deal with crooked pilots and evil pursuers. A solid sequel to *Airborn*.

180   Paolini, Christopher. *Eragon.*
    Knopf, 2004, ISBN 978-0-375-82668-9. 544p. **Series: Inheritance. ▪ Grades 5–8**

Eragon finds a beautiful blue stone, but before he can sell it, a dragon hatches from it. Eragon raises the dragon, Saphira, and becomes one of the last dragon riders. When Eragon and Saphira set out to avenge the murder of Eragon's uncle, they are caught in the middle of a fierce battle. As they struggle to decide which side they're on, Eragon learns about the world and his place in it. The second book in the series is *Eldest*.

181   Pearson, Ridley, and Dave Barry. *Peter and the Starcatchers.*
    Disney, 2004, ISBN 978-0-7868-5445-5. 464p. **Series: The Starcatchers. ▪ Grades 5–8**

Pearson and Barry provide their own "prequel" to the Peter Pan story. Readers will meet the familiar characters, as well as a few new ones. This is a fast-paced adventure that sets up the future adventures of Peter and his friends. Readers will enjoy the familiarity as well as the excitement of the adventures. There is a sequel to this book, *Peter and the Shadow Thieves* (2006)

182   Pullman, Phillip. *The Golden Compass.*
    Knopf, 1996, ISBN 978-0-679-87924-4. 416p. **Series: His Dark Materials. ▪ Grades 6–9**

Eleven-year-old Lyra goes on a quest to rescue her kidnapped friend Roger and her uncle, Lord Asriel. She has the help of a truth-telling instrument, an armored polar bear, and a Texan balloonist. She encounters both good and evil witches, and at one point nearly falls victim to evil experiments. The other books in the His Dark Materials trilogy are *The Subtle Knife* and *The Amber Spyglass*. *The Golden Compass* was made into a movie in 2007.

183   Reeve, Philip. *Mortal Engines.*
Eos, 2001, ISBN 978-0-06-008209-3. 373p. **Series: Hungry City Chronicles.** ▪ **Grades 8–11**

Tom is a fifteen-year-old apprentice living in a traction city. Traction cities are completely mobile cities that consume smaller cities in order to survive. When Tom is thrown from his city he is forced to survive on solid ground for the first time in his life. With a mysterious girl named Hester Shaw accompanying him, Tom discovers that his life is about to be changed drastically, and that his city's plan for survival threatens the world. It's up to Tom and Hester to save the world from his city's evil plan. This is the first book in the series. Other books in the series include *Predator's Gold*, *Infernal Devices*, and *A Darkling Plain*.

184   Rex, Adam. *The True Meaning of Smekday.*
Ill. by author. Hyperion, 2007, ISBN 978-0-7868-4900-0. 432p. ▪ **Grades 4–6**

Gratuity "Tip" Tucci is twelve years old and is working on a homework assignment called "The True Meaning of Smekday." Smekday is the day of celebration honoring when the earth was invaded by a race of aliens called the Boov. Tip writes of how she lost her mother and traveled the country looking for her, as well as how she befriended one of the Boov. She finally locates her mom and discovers the aliens have sinister plans for the planet and she must save the day. Although the main character is a girl, boys will enjoy the humor and the action as Tip travels the country on her own.

185   Riordan, Rick. *The Lightning Thief: Percy Jackson and the Olympians, Book 1.*
Miramax, 2005, ISBN 978-0-7868-5629-9. 377p. **Series: Percy Jackson and the Olympians.** ▪ **Grades 4–7**

Twelve-year-old Percy Jackson discovers the hard way that he's a demigod (half human and half god) when he's pursued by monsters. When he loses his mother on the way to Camp Half-Blood, his only haven, he makes friends with Grover (a young satyr) and Annabeth (the daughter of Athena). The three are thrown into a quest to find a missing lightning bolt that may cause the biggest war among the gods ever. This story is an exciting combination of Greek mythology and fantasy.

186   Riordan, Rick. *The Sea of Monsters: Percy Jackson and the Olympians, Book 2.*
    Miramax, 2006, ISBN 0-7868-5686-6. 279p. ▪ Grades 4–7

Percy Jackson and his friends Grover and Annabeth are back in the second book of this series. In this story Grover is in trouble on a quest. Camp Half-Blood is threatened and needs the Golden Fleece to stay secure. When the quest to retrieve the Golden Fleece is given to camp bully Clarisse, Percy decides to take matters into his own hands. This is another wild adventure featuring many monsters that would happily kill Percy. Action-filled pages will pull readers into this story.

187   Riordan, Rick. *Titan's Curse: Percy Jackson and the Olympians, Book 3.*
    Miramax, 2007, ISBN 978-1-4231-0145-1. 320p.
    ▪ Grades 4–7

Percy Jackson is now fourteen, and his best friend and sometime rival Annabeth is missing, as is Artemis, the goddess of the hunt. Percy and his friend Grover set out in search of Annabeth. In their adventures they encounter many friends and foes, including monsters intent on permanently ending Percy's journey. This third book in the series is action-packed and a masterful combination of Greek mythology and adventure.

188   Rowling, J. K. *Harry Potter and the Sorcerer's Stone.*
    Scholastic, 1998, ISBN 978-0-590-35340-3. 309p.
    ▪ Grades 3–6

It all started with this book. Harry Potter is a special orphan. Only he has been able to stop the evil Lord Voldemort, and the lightning scar on his forehead is evidence of that encounter. Harry learns about his wizarding heritage and is off for his first year at the wizarding school Hogwarts. There he encounters both friends and enemies as he learns more about the art and craft of magic. However, he also encounters his archenemy, Lord Voldemort, and must try to save the world of wizardry. The other books in the series are *Harry Potter and the Chamber of Secrets*, *Harry Potter and the Prisoner of Azkaban*, *Harry Potter and the Goblet of Fire*, *Harry Potter and the Order of the Phoenix*, *Harry Potter and the Half-Blood Prince*, and *Harry Potter and the Deathly Hallows*.

189   Sage, Angie. *Flyte: Septimus Heap.*
    Ill. by Mark Zug. Katherine Tegen Books, 2006, ISBN 978-0-06-057735-3. 532p. ▪ **Grades 5–7**

At the end of *Magyk*, the first book in the series (see below), Septimus Heap had become an apprentice to the ExtraOrdinary Wizard. This was very upsetting to his older brother Simon. Now Simon has become the apprentice of the evil necromancer DomDaniel. Simon's first task is to get rid of his "sister," the Princess Jenna. Jenna's kidnapping triggers a wild adventure for the other members of the Heap family as they try to rescue her and deal with their wayward son, Simon.

190   Sage, Angie. *Magyk: Septimus Heap.*
    Ill. by Mark Zug. Katherine Tegen Books, 2005, ISBN 978-0-06-057731-5. 564p. ▪ **Grades 5–7**

Septimus Heap is the seventh son of a seventh son. On the night he is born he is taken from his parents and they are told he has died. His father, Silas Heap, finds an abandoned baby girl in the snow that same night. The family takes her in and raises her as their own. On her tenth birthday they learn that she is a princess and that her life and theirs are in danger. When they flee for their safety, they discover the truth of what has happened to their son Septimus. Bonus features at the end of the book describe elements used in the fantasy genre. This series could be paired with Joseph Delaney's The Last Apprentice series (see entries 164–167).

191   Sage, Angie. *Physik: Septimus Heap.*

Ill. by Mark Zug. Katherine Tegen Books, 2007, ISBN 978-0-06-057737-7. 560p. ■ Grades 5–7

Septimus Heap has been spirited back in time by the great physician Marcellus Pye. Pye needs Septimus as an apprentice to help him create a new tincture that will provide him everlasting youth. Septimus's family, notably Princess Jenna, tries to find a way to go back in time to rescue Septimus. But Jenna's life is danger: The ghost of a former queen wants Jenna dead so she can usurp the throne. Many twists and turns await the reader in this third book in the series.

192   Shan, Darren. *Cirque Du Freak: A Living Nightmare.*

Little, Brown, 2004 pap., ISBN 978-0-316-90571-8. 384p. Series: Cirque Du Freak ■ Grades 5–7

Two boys sneak out of their houses one Saturday night to see a freak show in town. Enthralled by the show, Steve sneaks back later that night to steal Madame Octa (a giant spider) and teach her tricks. Steve enters into a freaky world indeed, and readers will be simultaneously captivated and uneasy. Fans of R. L. Stine will especially enjoy this series. Other books in the series include: *The Vampire's Assistant, Tunnels of Blood, Vampire Mountain, Trials of Death, Vampire Prince, Hunters of the Dusk, Allies of the Night,* and *Killers of the Dawn.*

193   Strickland, Brad. *The House Where Nobody Lived: A John Bellairs Mystery.*

Dial, 2006, ISBN 978-0-8037-3148-6. 173p. ■ Grades 4–6

Lewis Barnavelt and his best friend Rose stumble upon an abandoned but somehow well-kept house. They think nothing of it until they find out that the new boy at school is living in the house. When Lewis's sorcerer uncle and their neighbor check out the house, they find ghosts. Then Lewis sleeps at the house one night and an army of ghosts marches through. He alone must face them and send them back where they came from. Other recent titles in the Lewis Barnavelt series include *Ghost in the Mirror* and *The Whistle, the Grave, and the Ghost.*

Animal Fantasy

194   Avi. *Ragweed.*

Simon & Schuster, 2006 pap., ISBN 978-0-689-83721-0. 224p. **Series: Tales from Dimwood Forest.** ▪ **Grades 3–5**

Ragweed is a country mouse with big-city ambitions. When he sets out to seek adventure he ends up in a big town with a big cat. The big cat, Silversides, has started an organization called Felines Enraged About Rodents (FEAR). Ragweed meets many new friends in the town and unites the mice against Silversides in the book's exciting conclusion. This is the prequel to the Tales from Dimwood Forest series. The other books are *Poppy*, *Poppy and Rye*, *Poppy Returns*, and *Ereth's Birthday*.

195   Gleitzman, Morris. *Toad Rage.*

Putnam, 1999 pap., ISBN 0-14-130655-6. 151p.
▪ **Grades 4–6**

Limpy is a young Australian cane toad who can't understand why humans hate his species so much. He sets out on a quest to bridge the divide between humans and toads. He meets fellow animals and even Olympians who help him along his journey. This wild adventure that mixes animals and humans will appeal to readers who enjoy animal fantasy.

196   Jacques, Brian. *Redwall.*

Philomel, 1987, ISBN 978-0-399-21424-0. 352p.
▪ **Grades 4–7**

Redwall Abbey is a peaceful place where mice live quiet and happy lives. Cluny the Scourge, an evil rat, eyes the place and decides to invade. Martin the Warrior used to be the great defender of the abbey, but he's been gone a long time. Young Matthias takes on the challenge of being the abbey's brave warrior. Matthias learns quickly and discovers he may be the only one who can replace Martin. This action-packed animal fantasy series has many fans who enjoy cheering for Matthias. Other books in the series are *Mossflower*, *Mattimeo*, *Mariel of Redwall*, *Salamandastron*, *Martin of Redwall*, *The Bellmaker*, and *Outcast of Redwall*.

197   **Pratchett, Terry.** *The Amazing Maurice and His Educated Rodents.*
HarperCollins, 2001, ISBN 0-06-001233-1. 241p.
- Grades 4–6

In this fantasy version of the Pied Piper story, the rats and their leader, a cat, can think, act, and even speak for themselves. When they create a plan to take over a village by playing on humans' fear of rats, they discover a bigger problem in the village. Saving the day changes the relationship between rats and humans. This book will appeal to fans of Brian Jacques's *Redwall* (see above), and Avi's *Poppy* and *The Mayor of Central Park* (see entry 123).

198   **Hopkinson, Deborah.** *Sky Boys: How They Built the Empire State Building.*
Ill. by James Ransome. Schwartz & Wade, 2006, ISBN 978-0-375-83610-7. 48p.   ▪   Grades 2–4

The story of how the Empire State Building was constructed is told through the eyes of a young boy who visits the site each day. The fascinating story of how the landmark was built is complemented by the wonderful illustrations by Ransome. Author and illustrator notes at the end of the book will also intrigue readers.

199   **Polacco, Patricia.** *Pink and Say.*
Philomel, 1994, ISBN 978-0-399-22671-7. 48p.
- Grades 3–5

Sheldon Curtis (Say) is a fifteen-year-old white Civil War soldier who is badly wounded. Pinkus Aylee (Pink) is a black soldier about the same age. Pink finds Say and takes him home, where his mother nurses him back to health. Shortly after he's healed, Pink's mother is killed and the boys are captured. Pink is sentenced to be hanged, and the boys say good-bye in the gripping conclusion. An excellent, very powerful picture book.

Sources

Kiefer, B., Hickman, J., & Hepler S. (2006). *Charlotte Huck's Children's Literature*. McGraw-Hill.

Chapter 5

Historical Fiction

"Frequently the adventure stories could also be described as historical fiction; there is no clear division . . . " (Townsend, 1996). It has been established in a previous chapter that boys like adventure stories, and historical fiction is full of just that — adventure stories taking place in history. While this genre may not be as popular as it was in the past (Kiefer, Hepler, & Hickman, 2006), it is one that will attract boy readers because of the action-packed stories.

This chapter will expose readers to many different periods of time in history. Boys will be sucked into the stories, learning about key elements of historical time periods at the same time. This chapter is divided into two sections: Picture Books and Novels.

Picture Books

200   Smith, Lane. *John, Paul, George and Ben.*
Hyperion, 2006, ISBN 978-0-7868-4893-5. 32p.
- Grades 3–4

Smith illustrates humorous tales about five famous people in American history: John Hancock, Paul Revere, George Washington, Benjamin Franklin, and Thomas Jefferson. While the stories are more fiction than fact, a quiz at the end sets readers straight.

201   Yolen, Jane. *Encounter.*
Ill. by David Shannon. Harcourt, 1992, ISBN 978-0-15-
225962-4. 40p. ▪ **Grades 3–5**

This story imagines what the first meeting between Columbus and the
native people of San Salvador might have been like. The young native
narrator is apprehensive of the new visitors, yet his fears are ignored.
When some young people are captured after the first encounter, the
boy is able to escape and again voices his concerns, which fall on
deaf ears. Shannon's beautiful paintings accompany the text.

Novels

**202   Anderson, M. T. *The Astonishing Life of Octavian
Nothing, Traitor to the Nation: Volume I — The Pox
Party.***
Candlewick, 2006, ISBN 978-0-7636-2402-6. 368p.
▪ **Grades 8–12**
✪ **Michael Printz Honor Book, National Book Award Winner**

Octavian is a young black boy growing up in Boston just before the
American Revolution. He is the son of a "princess" yet is a scientific
experiment. When tensions rise with England and America decides to
revolt, things start to change for Octavian as he learns more about who
he is, where he's come from, and what future people have destined
for him. A challenging novel that deals with many issues. There is a
sequel to this book: *The Astonishing Life of Octavian Nothing, Traitor of a Nation: Volume II — The Kingdom on the Waves* (see below).

**203   Anderson, M. T. *The Astonishing Life of Octavian
Nothing, Traitor to the Nation: Volume II — The
Kingdom on the Waves.***
Candlewick, 2008, ISBN 978-0-7636-2950-2. ▪ **Grades 8–12**

Octavian is back and his adventures continue as he struggles for
freedom during a difficult time in America's history. Fans of the previous book (see above) will be excited to see what happens to Octavian and how he deals with the world around him.

204 Avi. *Crispin: At the Edge of the World.*

Hyperion, 2006, ISBN 978-0-7868-5152-2. 234p.
- Grades 5–7

Crispin and Bear are back in this sequel to *Crispin: The Cross of Lead* (see below), and Bear is still recovering from serious wounds. Continuing on the run (now from people who believe Bear has betrayed them), they are joined by a disfigured young girl named Troth. They locate a boat and travel across the Channel in hopes of finding freedom from their troubles. Crispin learns more about religion, war, and family in this fast-paced adventure.

205 Avi. *Crispin: The Cross of Lead.*

Hyperion, 2002, ISBN 978-0-7868-0828-1. 262p.
- Grades 5–7
- ✪ Newbery Medal

Young Crispin's mother has just died and the village has declared Crispin a "wolf's head," which means that anyone can kill him for a reward. Fleeing the village he stumbles across a big man named Bear, a juggler and entertainer. Bear takes young Crispin under his wing and together they travel the countryside of fourteenth-century England providing entertainment. Through their adventures Bear learns Crispin's true name and title, and Crispin starts to learn more about Bear. The conclusion is a suspenseful confrontation with those who have been pursuing the pair. The sequel is *Crispin: At the Edge of the World* (see above).

206 Avi. *Iron Thunder: The Battle Between the Monitor and the Merrimac.*

Hyperion, 2007, ISBN 978-1-4231-0446-9. 224p. **Series: I Witness.** ■ Grades 4–6

Tom Carroll's father is killed during the Civil War, and Tom, just thirteen, must find a job to support his family. When he becomes the assistant to a ship inventor he is immediately caught up in a web of war secrets, and his loyalties are tested. This is the first volume of a planned series that will combine history and adventure.

207   Bruchac, Joseph. *Code Talker.*

Dial, 2005, ISBN 978-0-8037-2921-6. 231p. ▪ **Grades 7–9**

Sixteen-year-old Ned Begay wants to be a part of the U.S. effort during World War II. He lies his way into the Marine Corps, claiming he's older than he is. After getting through boot camp easily, he's selected to join a top-secret group of "code talkers" who use the Navajo language to convey key information over the radio. Ned's adventures during the war are fascinating. Readers will be truly captivated by Bruchac's storytelling.

208   Choldenko, Gennifer. *Al Capone Does My Shirts.*

Putnam, 2004, ISBN 978-0-399-23861-1. 240p.
    ▪ **Grades 5–7**
    ✪ **Newbery Honor Book**

In 1935 Moose Flannigan and his family move to the island of Alcatraz, where his father obtains a job as an electrician and guard while his mother tries to get his autistic sister into a special school. It is hard for twelve-year-old Moose to adjust to life on the island. He has to take a boat to school each day and can't stay after school to play the sport he loves, baseball. Also, he must deal with the warden's daughter, who cooks up schemes (usually involving money) that get Moose into trouble. References to Al Capone add to the fun.

209   Chotjewitz, David. *Daniel, Half Human: And the Good Nazi.*

Trans. by Doris Orgel. Atheneum, 2004, ISBN 978-0-689-85747-8. 298p. ▪ **Grades 6–9**
    ✪ **Mildred L. Batchelder Honor Book**

Daniel is enjoying his life in Germany in 1933. He and his best friend, Armin, are excited about the rise of Hitler and are eager to join the Hitler Youth. But when thirteen-year-old Daniel finds out he is half Jewish (and thus, in his eyes, half human) his life changes drastically. Now he must struggle to survive, and his friendship with Armin is tested. A powerful novel and an excellent book to pair with *Hitler Youth* (see entry 340).

210 **Curtis, Christopher Paul.** *Bud, Not Buddy.*
Delacorte, 1999, ISBN 978-0-385-32306-2. 256p.
- ■ Grades 4–6
- ✪ Newbery Medal

Bud Caldwell is a ten-year-old streetwise orphan living during the Great Depression. He's tired of trying to fit in with different foster families. After he beats up his foster brother and is locked in a shed for the night, he sets out on his own. First he meets up with his "blood brother," Bugs, and then he decides to travel on foot across Michigan, from Flint to Grand Rapids, to find the man he believes to be his father. He is picked up by a caring man along the way, and finally comes face-to-face with a man who probably is not his father. Bud's sense of humor comes through and adds to the story's appeal.

211 **Curtis, Christopher Paul.** *Elijah of Buxton.*
Scholastic, 2007, ISBN 978-0-439-02344-3. 252p.
- ■ Grades 4–6
- ✪ Coretta Scott King Award, Newbery Honor Book

Eleven-year-old Elijah is born free during the time of slavery and lives in Canada across the border from Detroit, Michigan. He learns a lot about slavery as former slaves, both free, and escaped come to his town. When one steals money from his friend, Elijah pursues the thief into America, and his adventures begin. Curtis's other books include *The Watsons Go to Birmingham — 1963* (see below); *Bud, Not Buddy* (see above); and *Bucking the Sarge* (2004).

212 **Curtis, Christopher Paul.** *The Watsons Go to Birmingham — 1963.*
Delacorte, 1995, ISBN 978-0-385-32175-4. 224p.
- ■ Grades 4–6
- ✪ Newbery Honor Book; Coretta Scott King Honor Book

Kenny is one of the "Weird Watsons," as his African American family is known in Flint, Michigan. His southern-born mother doesn't cope well in the winter weather. His older brother Byron is slowly becoming a juvenile delinquent, and his parents decide that a family visit to their southern grandmother would do them all a lot of good. While they are down South they must confront racial issues, including a church bombing that threatens all of them. This powerful novel begins with humor and goes on to address serious issues of the South in the 1960s. Readers who like this book may also like *Bud, Not Buddy* (see above).

213   Dorros, Arthur. *Under the Sun.*
Amulet Books, 2004, ISBN 978-0-8109-4933-1. 224p.
 ▪ Grades 5–8

Thirteen-year-old Ehmet journeys across war-torn Bosnia. His destination may not even exist, as he's only heard rumors about a village of young people living peacefully. He encounters both friends and enemies as he struggles to find a new and peaceful home.

214   Durbin, William. *Broken Blade.*
Delacorte, 1997, ISBN 978-0-385-32224-9. 176p.
 ▪ Grades 4–6

After his father is severely injured chopping wood, thirteen-year-old Pierre takes his place as a canoeman. Pierre soon learns how demanding the job is, both physically and mentally. He has many adventures in this story set in nineteenth-century Canada. The sequel to this book is *Wintering* (see below).

215   Durbin, William. *Wintering.*
Delacorte, 1999, ISBN 978-0-385-32598-1. 208p.
 ▪ Grades 4–6

Pierre, the hero in Durbin's book *Broken Blade*, is back. Now he's fourteen and still working for a trading company. This time he helps set up a trading post in the French Canadian wilderness. Wintering at the new trading post means more exciting adventures for Pierre. Fans of the first book will enjoy this sequel.

216   Elliott, L. M. *Give Me Liberty.*
Katherine Tegen Books, 2006, ISBN 978-0-06-074421-2.
376p. ▪ Grades 4–6

Nathaniel Dunn is thirteen years old and an indentured servant. Things aren't looking good for him until in a stroke of luck he is sold and befriended by Basil, a schoolmaster who teaches Nathaniel about books, music, and more. When America starts to revolt against British rule, both Nathaniel and Basil must decide where they stand and what it will mean to fight for independence. This could be paired with M. T. Anderson's books about Octavian Nothing (see entries 202 and 203).

217   Fleischman, Paul. *Bull Run.*

Stan Clark Military Books, 1993, ISBN 978-0-06-021446-3. 104p. ▪ **Grades 4–6**

Sixteen chapters each present a different viewpoint of the first battle of the Civil War. This creative book offers the reader multiple perspectives of the same event.

218   Fleischman, Sid. *Bandit's Moon.*

Ill. by Jos. A. Smith. Greenwillow, 1998, ISBN 978-0-688-15830-9. 144p. ▪ **Grades 4–6**

Annyrose feels as if she's being held captive by the evil O. O. Mary. O. O. Mary is supposed to take care of her while her brother is away making his fortune during the Gold Rush. When bandits arrive at O. O. Mary's place they mistake Annyrose for a boy (her hair is very short). The notorious Joaquin Murieta carries her off in hopes that she will teach him to read. During her time with the bandits Annyrose learns just what led them to a life of crime and tries to turn them to good. A fast-paced, humorous adventure.

219   Fleischman, Sid. *The Entertainer and the Dybbuk.*

Greenwillow, 2007, ISBN 978-0-06-134445-9. 180p. ▪ **Grades 5–7**

The Great Freddie is a mediocre ventriloquist touring Europe after World War II. He becomes possessed by a dybbuk (a Jewish spirit). The dybbuk now does the talking for the Great Freddie and turns him into the best ventriloquist ever. But the dybbuk has a plan—to seek revenge on the German soldier who killed him years before. The spirit uses the stage as his means to find the man who killed him, causing problems for Freddie in his professional and personal lives. Fleischman has masterfully combined fantasy and history in this story about the aftermath of the Holocaust.

220 **Fleischman, Sid.** *The Giant Rat of Sumatra: Or Pirates Galore.*
Ill. by John Hendrix. Greenwillow, 2005, ISBN 978-0-06-074238-6. 208p. ▪ **Grades 5–7**

A cabin boy named Shipwreck arrives in San Diego in 1846 with Captain Gallows. Shipwreck would love to return to his home in New England, but cannot find passage on a ship. Instead he stays to help Captain Gallows "settle down" after life on the high seas. But life is far from peaceful when Shipwreck and the captain are confronted by bandits. The lead bandit turns out to be someone from Captain Gallows's past. A fast-paced adventure with good humor.

221 **Fleischman, Sid.** *The Thirteenth Floor: A Ghost Story.*
Greenwillow, 1995, ISBN 978-0-688-14216-2. 144p.
▪ **Grades 4–6**

At age twelve, Buddy has just lost his parents and must go live with his sister, a high-powered attorney. When she leaves a cryptic message on her apartment's answering machine about an elevator and the thirteenth floor, Buddy sets off to find her. The thirteenth floor turns out to be a time slip that allows Buddy to travel to the seventeenth century. There he connects with Captain Crackstone, rumored to be a pirate. While trying to find his sister, Buddy learns what life was like in the seventeenth century and what led to the Salem witch trials.

222 **Karr, Kathleen.** *The Great Turkey Walk.*
Farrar, Straus & Giroux, 1998, ISBN 978-0-374-32773-6. 208p. ▪ **Grades 4–6**

In 1860, Simon Green has just completed third grade for the fourth time and is now fifteen years old. His teacher decides that maybe school isn't the place for Simon. Simon comes up with a business venture. Turkeys are worth twenty-five cents in Missouri, where he lives, and five dollars in Denver. Simon's idea is to buy a flock of 1,000 turkeys, walk them to Denver, and become a very rich man. With a loan from his teacher, he sets forth on this adventure. This funny novel is worth reading aloud.

223   Napoli, Donna Jo. *Fire in the Hills.*
Yearling, 2006, ISBN 978-0-525-47751-8. 256p.
▪ **Grades 5–8**

Roberto, only fifteen years old, is struggling to return to his Venice home in the middle of World War II. Having already survived an injury, he is captured a second time by the Germans. This time they use him as a translator. He eventually escapes. On his journey home he encounters other youths who are part of the resistance and who provide ammunition and food to those in need. Roberto feels good about doing his part but continues to long for his home. Finally, as the war ends, Roberto finds himself on the road home. Readers who enjoy Roberto's story may like the prequel, *Stones in Water*.

224   Napoli, Donna Jo. *The King of Mulberry Street.*
Yearling, 2007, ISBN 978-0-553-49416-7. 245p.
▪ **Grades 5–7**

Beniamino is a nine-year-old boy living in Naples, Italy. When his mother decides she can no longer support him, she smuggles him onto a ship bound for America. When Beniamino discovers that his mother is not on board, he realizes he must fend for himself. On landing in New York City, Beniamino finds that survival will be much more challenging than he thought. He befriends two other homeless boys and starts his own business. As he begins to prosper Beniamino finds that perhaps his new home is a better place for him than Naples. This is a very well told story.

225   Newton, Robert. *Runner.*
Knopf, 2007, ISBN 978-0-375-83744-9. 209p. ▪ **Grades 7–9**

Living in poverty in Melbourne, Australia, in 1919, fifteen-year-old Charlie decides he's had enough of school and wants to help support his family. He decides to start working for a mob boss named Squizzy Taylor. But as he makes "runs" for Squizzy, he decides maybe this isn't the life for him. Charlie has always loved running, and decides to enter running competitions for cash. These competitions lead to an exciting conclusion. A glossary at the end of the book will help readers understand new vocabulary.

226   Park, Linda Sue. *A Single Shard.*
       Clarion, 2001, ISBN 978-0-395-97827-6. 160p.
       ■ Grades 5–7
       ✪ Newbery Medal

Young Tree-Ear, an orphan, is cared for by a homeless man in a village of potters in twelfth-century Korea. Tree-Ear especially admires the work of the potter Min. When Tree-Ear accidentally drops one of Min's pieces he works for Min to pay off the debt. He stays on long after the debt is paid in hopes of becoming a fine potter like Min. Tree-Ear is then given the important task of taking some of Min's pieces to the king. On this long hard journey Tree-Ear learns the value of courage.

227   Paterson, Katherine. *Jip: His Story.*
       Scholastic, 1997, ISBN 978-0-590-26328-3. 181p.
       ■ Grades 5–7

Young Jip was abandoned as a child and in 1855 he's living on a "poor farm." Here it is discovered that he has a gift for dealing with wild beasts. The town brings a lunatic to the poor farm in hopes that Jip can help him. Through working with the lunatic, Jip learns more about his own past and his family. Eventually both catch up with him and Jip must go on the run to survive. A creative story with twists and turns and a very subtle connection to another Paterson book, *Lyddie* (1991).

228   Paulsen, Gary. *Call Me Francis Tucket.*
       Delacorte, 1995, ISBN 978-0-385-32116-7. 112p. **Series:**
       Tucket. ■ Grades 4–6

In this sequel to *Mr. Tucket* (see below), Francis sets out on his own. Two orphaned children join him as he works his way west. Many challenges await him in the Wild West, and with two children in tow the struggles are harder. This is a good series that can motivate reluctant readers, engaging them with fast-paced action.

229   Paulsen, Gary. *Mr. Tucket.*
       Delacorte, 1994, ISBN 978-0-385-31169-4. 176p. **Series:**
       Tucket. ■ Grades 4–6

Francis Tucket and his family are following the Oregon Trail to a new life. Francis falls behind the wagon train while shooting cow pies with the rifle he received for his fourteenth birthday. Suddenly he's captured by the Pawnee tribe and taken to live with them. Francis sees a one-armed white man, Mr. Grimes, in the village, and sends him secret pleas for help. Mr. Grimes helps him escape and teaches him how to survive in the Wild West. While Francis is grateful for the rescue and all he's learned, he longs to reunite with his family. The Tucket books include *Call Me Francis Tucket* (see above), *Tucket's Ride*, *Tucket's Gold* (see below), and *Tucket's Home*.

230   Paulsen, Gary. *Tucket's Gold.*
Delacorte, 1999, ISBN 978-0-385-32501-1. 112p. **Series: Tucket.** ▪ **Grades 4–6**

This is the fourth book in the Tucket series. Francis, fifteen years old, is traveling with two "adopted" orphans, Lottie and Sam. They are still on the run from the Commancheros, a group of ruthless men who want to sell the children into slavery. Francis and the children find hidden gold and are captured by outlaws. Readers will enjoy the familiarity of the series and the adventure found within these pages.

231   Peck, Richard. *Fair Weather.*
Dial, 2001, ISBN 978-0-8037-2516-4. 2001p. ▪ **Grades 5–7**

Rosie Beckett and her family are invited to visit her rich Aunt Euterpe in Chicago, site of the 1893 world's fair. Rosie's mother accepts the offer, even though she has always told thirteen-year-old Rosie and her younger brother that Chicago is full of criminals. While in Chicago the family scares off the aunt's hired help and embarrasses her in front of her socialite friends. But they get to go to the world's fair and uncover a fun secret about their grandfather at the same time. Peck's storytelling flair and humor come through beautifully.

232   Peck, Richard. *Here Lies the Librarian.*
Dial, 2006, ISBN 978-0-8037-3080-9. 160p. ▪ **Grades 5–7**

It's rural Indiana in 1914 and PeeWee is living with her older brother Jake. They run a small garage on the outskirts of town. After the town librarian dies it is decided to close the library, but four wealthy Butler University students with degrees in library science want to reopen it. In the students PeeWee finds friendship away from the greasy cars she loves to fix. This is fast-paced and funny, and the car race at the end adds to the enjoyment.

233   Peck, Richard. *A Long Way From Chicago.*

Dial, 1998, ISBN 978-0-8037-2290-3. 192p. ▪ Grades 4–7
✪ Newbery Honor Book

Joe Dowdel tells of one summer in the 1930s when he and his sister visited their grandmother in small-town Illinois. The two children see how their crafty grandmother uses humor (and sometimes intimidation or manipulation) to help others, and appreciate this different side of her. Each incident is funnier than the last and Grandmother's spirit shows in her antics. The sequel, *A Year Down Yonder*, is equally funny and is a Newbery Medal winner.

234   Peck, Richard. *On the Wings of Heroes.*

Dial, 2007, ISBN 978-0-8037-3081-6. 160p. ▪ Grades 4–6

Davy Bowman narrates this story about his American family coping with World War II at home. His older brother has enlisted and is fighting overseas, and Davy and his buddy work to gather scrap metal, newspapers, milkweed, and other items to help support the war effort. Davy describes the fun he had growing up during that time. Readers will enjoy his anecdotes and learn some history.

235   Peck, Richard. *The Teacher's Funeral: A Comedy in Three Parts.*

Dial, 2004, ISBN 978-0-8037-2736-6. 208p. ▪ Grades 5–7

"If your teacher has to die, August isn't a bad time of year for it," says Russell, who in 1904 is fifteen years old. While saddened by the death of his teacher, he's ecstatic at the thought of the school board being unable to replace her. When his older sister fills in (even though she herself has one year of school left) Russell's nightmare has come true. This is a comical account of Russell's year of being taught by his sister.

236 Peet, Mal. *Tamar: A Novel of Espionage, Passion, and Betrayal.*

Candlewick, 2007, ISBN 978-0-7636-3488-9. 432p.
- Grades 8–12
- ✪ Carnegie Medal

This young adult novel tells two stories simultaneously. The original story takes place during World War II in the Netherlands as resistance fighters struggle against the Nazi regime. One of the fighter's granddaughters, Tamar, tells the second story after her grandfather leaves her a mysterious box when he dies. In the box are mysteries that unravel as she learns more about what happened during the war.

237 Schmidt, Gary D. *Lizzie Bright and the Buckminster Boy.*

Clarion, 2004, ISBN 978-0-618-43929-4. 224p.
- Grades 6–9
- ✪ Michael Printz Honor Award; Newbery Honor Book

Thirteen-year-old Turner is a preacher's son in 1912. When he and his father arrive in a small town in Maine, he hates the town immediately. Things change a bit when Turner is befriended by Lizzie Bright Griffin, a girl who also happens to be the first African American he has ever met. This friendship meets with disapproval from both Turner's father and the town's elders. When Turner gets in trouble and is forced to visit an elderly woman, Lizzie joins him. A friendship is forged by all three, although lives are changed forever, and Turner must decide if and how he will stand up to the racism in his new town.

238 Schmidt, Gary D. *The Wednesday Wars.*

Clarion, 2007, ISBN 978-0-618-72483-3. 272p.
- Grades 6–9
- ✪ Newbery Honor Book

Holling is the only Presbyterian in his seventh-grade class. The rest of his classmates are Catholic and Jewish, and attend religious classes in the afternoons. Holling is stuck alone with his teacher, Mrs. Baker, all afternoon. He believes she intentionally tortures him by making him read *and* discuss Shakespeare all afternoon. Yet Holling learns a lot about his teacher and about himself as well as about growing up in the 1960s in New York. Schmidt is also the author of *Lizzie Bright and the Buckminster Boy* (see entry 237).

239 Weaver, Will. *Full Service.*
Farrar, Straus & Giroux, 2005, ISBN 978-0-374-32485-8.
240p. ■ **Grades 7–10**

Fifteen-year-old Paul Sutton gets a summer job working at a gas station during the mid-1960s. There's a lot going on in the country at this time, and Paul gets to see it all at his new job. From bamboozlers to pretty girls to hippies, as well as drugs and alcohol, Paul's worldview gets widened. Boys will be drawn to all the different things Paul sees each day. Weaver has a great storytelling voice that will appeal to readers.

Sources

Kiefer, B., Hickman, J., & Hepler S. (2006). *Charlotte Huck's Children's Literature*. McGraw-Hill.

Chapter 6

Poetry

"Reading a poem should not be like performing an autopsy, looking at a dead object and figuring out what killed it. Or, worse, trying to figure out what it might have been like when it was alive. Good poems *are* alive . . . " (Janeczko, 2003). Poetry and boys — they *can* go together. Many wonderful children's poems appeal to boy readers. When boys discover that good poetry is alive, as Janeczko writes, they will be drawn to this genre.

Shel Silverstein and Jack Prelutsky are two examples of accessible poets, but one of my goals for this chapter is to take boy readers beyond Silverstein and Prelutsky, whom they may discover on their own. The titles found in this chapter include funny and serious poems about sports, animals, nature, and everyday life. Readers who enjoy these poems will also like these novels in verse, found in Chapter 2: Jaime Adoff's *Jimi and Me*, Sharon Creech's *Love that Dog*, Mel Glenn's *Jump Ball!* and *Who Killed Mr. Chippendale?*, and Nikki Grimes's *Bronx Masquerade*. And, readers who find poetry difficult may appreciate it more if they read the novels first.

240   **Adoff, Jaime. *The Song Shoots Out of My Mouth: A Celebration of Music.***
       Dutton, 2002, ISBN 0-525-46949-4. 48p. ■ **Grades 4–7**
Poetry and music are a perfect match, and Adoff proves it in this book. Poems about instruments, musicians, and forms of music will

lure readers into both poetry and music. In one poem, Adoff captures the joy of singing: "My throat the Cape Canaveral of my soul. . . ."

241   Collier, Bryan. *Uptown.*
Holt, 2000, ISBN 978-0-8050-5721-8. 32p. ▪ Grades 2–4
✪ Coretta Scott King Award

A young boy describes living "uptown" in New York City's Harlem. He relishes the familiar sights of the Hudson river, the barbershop, the brownstones, the musicians. Readers will see Harlem through the eyes of a boy with a loving imagination.

242   Fleischman, Paul. *Big Talk: Poems for Four Voices.*
Ill. by Beppe Giacobbe. Candlewick, 2000, ISBN 978-0-7636-0636-7. 48p. ▪ Grades 3–5

Fleischman's first books of poetry were for two voices. Now he's doubled the number and these poems can be read by four. These more complex poems describe night sounds, school gossip, and wistful ghosts. The poet provides explanations of how the poems should be read.

243   Florian, Douglas. *Comets, Stars, the Moon, and Mars: Space Poems and Paintings.*
Ill. by author. Harcourt, 2007, ISBN 978-0-15-205372-7. 48p.
▪ Grades 3–5

Florian usually writes poems about animals. In this collection he travels into space and beyond: "The universe is every place / Including all the empty space / It's every star and galaxy / All objects of astronomy, /geography, zoology/(each cat and dog and bumblebee) . . . ."

244   Florian, Douglas. *Mammalabilia.*
Ill. by author. Harcourt, 2000, ISBN 0-15-202167-1. 48p.
▪ Grades 2–5

Simple poems explore the use of rhyme to describe well-known animals. About aardvarks, he writes: "Aardvarks aare odd / Aardvarks aare staark / Aardvarks look better / By faar in the daark." Florian's creative illustrations add to the reader's enjoyment.

245   Florian, Douglas. *Omnibeasts.*

Ill. by author. Harcourt, 2004, ISBN 0-15-205038-8. 95p.
- Grades 3–6

Florian writes about some of his favorite animals in this collection of poems, several of which can be found in his previous books. The illustrations add to the appeal.

246   Florian, Douglas. *Zoo's Who.*

Ill. by author. Harcourt, 2005, ISBN 0-15-204639-9. 48p.
- Grades 2–5

In this book Florian takes the reader to the zoo. Each poem is about a different animal or insect that a visitor to the zoo might see.

247   Greenberg, David. *Bugs!*

Ill. by Lynn Munsinger. Little, Brown, 2002, ISBN 978-0-316-35576-6. 32p. ▪ Grades 2–4

Boys and bugs always make a great combination. This book of nonsense poetry is sure to delight young boy readers (and most likely disgust adults). Fun illustrations complement the poems.

248   Greenfield, Eloise. *For the Love of the Game: Michael Jordan and Me.*

Ill. by Jan Spivey Gilchrist. HarperCollins, 1997, ISBN 978-0-06-027298-2. 32p. ▪ Grades 3–5

"When he was just a little boy / when he was just a kid / Michael saw a basketball / and this is what he did." This inspirational book is about overcoming life's struggles. Using Michael Jordan as a model, Greenfield's words encourage readers to be the best that they can be. Beautiful illustrations accompany the verse.

249   Grimes, Nikki. *My Man Blue: Poems.*

Ill. by Jerome Lagarrigue. Putnam, 1999, ISBN 978-0-8037-2326-9. 32p. ▪ Grades 3–5

Damon is a young boy without a father. When he meets Blue, a rough-looking friend of his mother's, he's suspicious at first. But a friendship slowly grows between Damon and Blue. "Second Son" reveals that Blue hopes to be a father to Damon, and each following poem shows how Blue keeps his word. A touching look at the importance of fathers in African American life.

250   Grossman, Bill. *My Little Sister Ate One Hare.*
Ill. by Kevin Hawkes. Dragonfly, 1998, ISBN 978-0-517-88576-5. 32p. ▪ **Grades 2–4**

A poetry book and counting book in one. The narrator's little sister will eat anything but nutritious food: "My little sister ate 3 ants / She even ate their underpants / She ate 2 snakes, she ate 1 hare. / We thought she'd throw up then and there. / But she didn't."

251   Grossman, Bill. *My Little Sister Hugged an Ape.*
Ill. by Kevin Hawkes. Knopf, 2004, ISBN 978-0-517-80017-1. 40p. ▪ **Grades 2–4**

The little sister is back! She zealously hugs animals from A to Z, even the prickly, the slimy, and the scary. The slightly yucky humor and outrageous illustrations add to the fun.

252   Grossman, Bill. *Timothy Tunny Swallowed a Bunny.*
Ill. by Kevin Hawkes. Laura Geringer Books, 2000, ISBN 978-0-06-028758-0. 32p. ▪ **Grades 2–4**

Timothy is just one of the characters found in unusual situations in this collection of zany, snappy verse. There's Ned, with a horse on his head; Walter Lackwards, whose head is on backwards; and plenty of other goofy folks, all brought to life by the artwork of Kevin Hawkes.

253   Hopkins, Lee Bennett. *Oh, No! Where Are My Pants? And Other Disasters: Poems.*
Ill. by Wolf Erlbruch. HarperCollins, 2005, ISBN 0-688-17860-X. 32p. ▪ **Grades 3–5**

This humorous collection of poems selected by Lee Bennett Hopkins is sure to make boys laugh. Poems about the struggles and joys of being a child will entertain readers. Susan Hart Lindquist's "First Day" describes being separated from a friend: "This isn't the way it was supposed to be — You in Room Two. Me in Room Three."

254   Janeczko, Paul. *A Kick in the Head: An Everyday Guide to Poetic Forms.*

Ill. by Chris Raschka. Candlewick, 2005, ISBN 0-7636-0662-6. 61p. ▪ Grades 4–7

This is the book to introduce different forms of poetry. Raschka's illustrations highlight the poems that Janeczko has selected. They present more than 20 different forms of poetry with fun illustrations to complement them.

255   Janeczko, Paul. *A Poke in the Eye: A Collection of Concrete Poems.*

Ill. by Chris Raschka. Candlewick, 2001, ISBN 0-7636-0661-8. 36p. ▪ Grades 3–6

This book of concrete poems shows how poetry and art can come together. Author and illustrator cover a wide range of topics, from a poem in eye chart format to a poem about tennis.

256   Janeczko, Paul. *That Sweet Diamond: Baseball Poems.*

Ill. by Carole Katchen. Atheneum, 1998, ISBN 0-689-80735-X. 48p. ▪ Grades 3–6

There is just as much focus on the fans as on the players in these poems about the magic of a baseball game. "Things to Do During a Rain Delay" has suggestions on how to pass the time; other poems are about spitting, the trials of being a catcher, and the devotion of lifelong fans.

257   Kennedy, X. J. *Exploding Gravy: Poems to Make You Laugh.*

Ill. by Joy Allen. Little, Brown, 2002, ISBN 978-0-316-38423-0. 128p. ▪ Grades 2–5

In this collection X. J. Kennedy gives readers plenty to laugh about. Zany poems in all forms about monsters, dinosaurs, quirky family members, favorite foods, and more will appeal to boys with a sense of humor.

258 **Korman, Gordon, and Bernice Korman.** *The D Poems of Jeremy Bloom: A Collection of Poems About School, Homework, and Life (Sort Of).*

Apple, 1992, ISBN 0-590-44819-6. 97p. ▪ **Grades 4–7**

Perhaps his English teacher summed it up best for Jeremy Bloom: "Anyone who sees 'pottery' instead of 'poetry' deserves all the English classes he can get." So begins the school year for Jeremy, as he learns not only to read poetry but to write it as well. The poems are quite funny as he experiments with words and describes the details of his life.

259 **Korman, Gordon, and Bernice Korman.** *The Last-Place Sports Poems of Jeremy Bloom: A Collection of Poems About Winning, Losing, and Being a Good Sport (Sometimes).*

Scholastic, 1996, ISBN 0-590-25516-9. 92p. ▪ **Grades 4–7**

Jeremy Bloom is back, and so is his poetry. In this sequel to his first collection of poems, Jeremy writes about his favorite topic: sports. Author Gordon Korman and his mother Bernice are at it again, coming up with hysterically funny poems. This is a great collection for anyone who enjoys humorous poetry.

260 **Lewis, J. Patrick.** *Arithme-tickle: An Even Number of Odd Riddle-Rhymes.*

Ill. by Frank Remkiewicz. Voyager, 2007, ISBN 978-0-15-205848-7. 32p. ▪ **Grades 2–3**

Poetry and math . . . can the two be combined? J. Patrick Lewis shows they can. He creates whimsical rhymes that teach math skills. The illustrations add to the poems' humor.

261 **Lewis, J. Patrick.** *Doodle Dandies: Poems That Take Shape.*

Ill. by Lisa Desimini. Aladdin, 2002, ISBN 978-0-689-84889-6. 40p. ▪ **Grades 2–3**

Younger readers will enjoy these poems that echo the shapes of their subjects. Umbrellas, budding flowers, baseballs, skyscrapers, and comets take shape in words.

262   Lewis, J. Patrick. *Riddle-icious.*
Ill. by Debbie Tilley. Dragonfly, 1997, ISBN 978-0-679-88545-0. 32p. ▪ **Grades 2–3**

This is a fun collection of wordplay poems. Tilley's illustrations camouflage the answers. Readers will learn new words as they solve the riddles.

263   Lewis, J. Patrick. *Riddle-Lightful: Oodles of Little Riddle Poems.*
Knopf, 1998, ISBN 978-0-679-88760-7. 32p. ▪ **Grades 3–5**

Boys will enjoy the challenge of each of these thirty-two riddle-poems. Plenty of clues will help them solve the riddles about familiar objects.

264   Matott, Justin. *There's a Fly on My Toast.*
Ill. by John Woods Jr.. Clove Pubns, 2002, ISBN 978-1-889191-23-2. 130p. ▪ **Grades 3–5**

What should you do if a fly lands on your toast? If you discover your elbows are wrinkly? This clever book of poems addresses everyday and out-of-the-ordinary situations and features cartoonish illustrations.

265   Montes, Marisa. *Los Gatos Black on Halloween.*
Ill. by Yuyi Morales. Holt, 2006, ISBN 978-0-8050-7429-1. 32p. ▪ **Grades 2–4**

This poem about one Halloween night with ghosts, witches, graves, and monsters will spook many readers. Spanish words are interspersed throughout the text with a glossary at the end. Readers will enjoy the creepy illustrations. A wonderful bilingual Halloween poem.

266   Myers, Walter Dean. *Blues Journey.*
Ill. by Christopher Myers. Holiday House, 2003, ISBN 978-0-82342-079-7. 32p. ▪ **Grades 4–6**

Walter Dean Myers and his son Christopher collaborated to produce this beautifully illustrated poetry book. This book has a bluesy feel to it through the use of the verse, which covers some very serious issues. Readers will enjoy the music of the words while their eyes are drawn to the spectacular illustrations.

267   Myers, Walter Dean. *Harlem: A Poem.*

Ill. by Christopher Myers. Scholastic, 1997, ISBN 978-0-590-54340-8. 32p. ▪ **Grades 3–6**

✪ **Coretta Scott King Honor Book, Caldecott Honor Book**

This is an excellent picture book that is one complete poem. Myers, with the help of his son's illustrations, captures the sights, sounds, joys, and injustices of Harlem, New York. This collection is suited to older readers who have been introduced to the issues faced by African Americans.

268   Myers, Walter Dean. *Here in Harlem: Poems in Many Voices.*

Holiday House, 2004, ISBN 978-0-8234-1853-4. 88p.

▪ **Grades 6–9**

Myers presents another view of Harlem in this book, a fresh collection of poems for many voices. Readers can choose to read independently, with a partner, or to listen to the words as they come off the page in a bluesy song.

269   Nelson, Marilyn. *A Wreath for Emmett Till.*

Houghton Mifflin, 2005, ISBN 978-0-618-39752-5. 48p.

▪ **Grades 9–12**

This book is about the horrific lynching of Emmett Till in 1955. The last line of one poem is the first line of the next, and the first line of each poem creates the fifteenth poem. Disturbing and reflective, it's a powerful book detailing different perspectives of the crime. Consider pairing this with Chris Crowe's *Getting Away with Murder* (see entry 342).

270   Noda, Takayo. *Dear World.*

Putnam, 2005, ISBN 978-0-14-240280-1. 32p. ▪ **Grades 2–3**

This is a nice collection of gentle, short poems describing items in a child's life. Each poem is a loving letter, whether to a tree, a flower, the ocean, or another part of the small child's world. The author's collages add to the dreamy feel of the book.

271   Scieszka, Jon. *Science Verse.*

Ill. by Lane Smith. Viking, 2004, ISBN 978-0-670-91057-1. 42p. ▪ Grades 3–5

The hysterically funny sequel to *Math Curse* (1995). "I think that I ain't ever seen / A poem ugly as a spleen," begins one poem. Did the dinosaurs die of boredom? Did Mary have not a little lamb, but parasites? Zapped with a curse, a student ponders science. An included CD features Scieszka and Smith reading the poems, which are set to familiar tunes and verses such as "The Battle Hymn of the Republic" and "Jabberwocky."

272   Soto, Gary. *Fearless Fernie: Hanging Out with Fernie and Me.*

Ill. by Regan Dunnick. Putnam, 2002, ISBN 978-0-399-23615-0. 64p. ▪ Grades 4–6

A collection of forty-one poems told from the perspective of two sixth-grade boys. Each poem tackles the struggles the characters have had in growing up. Sometimes funny, sometimes serious, the poems will help boys realize they are not alone in the challenges they face.

273   Steptoe, Javako. *In Daddy's Arms I Am Tall: African Americans Celebrating Fathers.*

Lee & Low, 1997, ISBN 978-1-880000-31-1. 32p. ▪ Grades 3–5

This book is a collection of thirteen poems by various poets, all describing African American fathers. Steptoe's beautiful collage illustrations accompany the poems, adding to the power of each one.

274   Wolf, Allan. *Blood-Hungry Spleen: And Other Poems About Our Parts.*

Ill. by Greg Clarke. Candlewick, 2003, ISBN 0-7636-1565-X. 56p. ▪ Grades 4–8

Tongues, bones, belly buttons . . . this book is composed of different poems about the human body. Some are serious, and some are quite comical. The title alone will draw boys to the book.

275 Woodson, Jacqueline. *Locomotion.*
Scholastic, 2003, ISBN 0-439-63615-9. 100p. ▪ Grades 4–6
✪ Coretta Scott King Author Honor Book

Lonnie and his sister lose their parents in a fire. Through different poetic styles (sonnet, haiku, and others) introduced by his teacher, Lonnie tells about being apart from his sister, who is living with a different foster family. Lonnie describes the struggles of fitting in at a new home and at school. A very powerful story told in poems.

276 Yolen, Jane. *Snow, Snow: Winter Poems for Children.*
Ill. by Jason Stemple. Boyds Mills, 1998, ISBN 978-1-56397-721-3. 32p. ▪ Grades 3–4

Yolen writes vivid verse about the cold season, and her son Jason's photographs add to each poem. The joys and beauty of snow are captured well. Readers who enjoy Jane Yolen's poems and Jason's photographs will want to also check out *Color Me a Rhyme*, *Fine Feathered Friends*, *Horizons*, *Least Things*, and *Wild Things*.

277 Zahares, Wade. *Big, Bad, and a Little Bit Scary: Poems That Bite Back!*
Ill. by author. Viking, 2001, ISBN 978-0-670-03513-7. 32p.
▪ Grades 2–4

Beware scary animals that bite! Vipers, eels, piranhas, and other fierce creatures grace the pages of this collection of poems.

Sources

Janeczko, Paul B. (2003). *Opening a Door: Reading Poetry in the Middle School Classroom*. Scholastic.

Chapter 7

Graphic Novels

Graphic novels are generating a lot of buzz. No matter what is said about the genre, there's no denying that the comic-book format appeals to readers. As Cary writes in *Going Graphic* (2004), "If you ask students at various grade levels why they like comics, one word keeps popping up over and over again: fun. It's a word that makes for brain engagement and a word I wish I heard more often in the schools when we talk about academic curriculum."

To me the graphic novel is all about format. It looks like a comic book, but reading it is much more complex. How do the illustrations work with the text to tell the story? What do readers need to do to comprehend the text? The illustrations in a graphic novel can be quite complex and truly challenge the reader, even with little text (or no text, see *The Arrival, Shaun Tan*). The main advantage to graphic novels is that this format is motivating male readers.

With so many new graphic novels being published, it's important for us to be aware of what's available. For this chapter I've included titles that will appeal to readers of all ages, from preschoolers to young adults. Note: Be sure to preview titles so that you're aware of the more serious content found in some graphic novels for older readers. This chapter is divided into five sections: Simple Picture Books, More-Complex Picture Books, Partial Graphic Novels, Graphic Novels for Younger Readers, and Graphic Novels for Young Adults.

Simple Picture Books

278 Cosentino, Ralph. *The Marvelous Misadventures of Fun-Boy.*

Ill. by author. Viking, 2006, ISBN 978-0-670-05961-4. 32p.
- **Grades 2–3**

Fun-Boy is a wordless picture book in comic-book format. Each double-page spread is a mini-story in four frames. Readers must pay close attention to each picture to pick up subtle changes that influence the story.

279 Debon, Nicolas. *The Strongest Man in the World: Louis Cyr.*

Ill. by author. Groundwood, 2007, ISBN 978-0-88899-731-9. 32p. ■ **Grades 3–5**

In the early 1900s, Louis Cyr, "the strongest man in the world," is told he must retire. Saddened by this, he begins to tell his daughter about the adventures he has had. In the end Louis decides he prefers the adoration of his daughter to that of the crowds he used to please.

280 Kitamura, Satoshi. *Comic Adventures of Boots.*

Ill. by author. Farrar, Straus & Giroux, 2002, ISBN 978-0-374-31455-2. 32p. ■ **Grades 2–3**

Three different adventures of a cat named Boots. Each story is told using comic-book frames. Readers — even reluctant ones — will enjoy the humorous stories as well as the art. Kitamura has also written *A Friend for Boots* and *Bath-Time Boots*.

281 O'Connor, George. *Kapow!*

Ill. by author. Simon & Schuster, 2004, ISBN 978-0-689-86718-7. 32p. ■ **Grades 2–3**

A little boy imagines himself as the superhero "American Eagle." The imaginary adventures that he and his friends have make a big mess in the real world. The illustrations incorporate comic-book and graphic-novel elements into a picture book.

282   O'Connor, George. *Ker-Splash!*

Ill. by author. Simon & Schuster, 2005, ISBN 978-0-689-87682-0. 32p. ▪ **Grades 2–3**

"Superhero" American Eagle is back! And now one of his superhero friends joins him on a trip to the beach. They encounter trouble and come to the rescue using their superpowers. O'Connor again does a nice job of combining comic-book and graphic-novel elements into a picture book. A fun sequel for fans of *Kapow!* (see above).

283   O'Malley, Kevin. *Captain Raptor and the Moon Mystery.*

Ill. by Patrick O'Brien. Walker, 2005, ISBN 978-0-8027-8935-8. 32p. ▪ **Grades 3–4**

When a UFO crashes into his planet, Captain Raptor (a dinosaur astronaut) must investigate the craft. He rescues a human space traveler and helps to get him back on his journey. Comic-book and graphic-novel elements tell the story. A sequel is *Captain Raptor and the Space Pirates* (2007).

284   Spiegelman, Art, and Françoise Mouly, eds. *It Was a Dark and Silly Night.*

Joanna Cotler Books, 2003, ISBN 978-0-06-028628-6. 48p. ▪ **Grades 3–5**

Twelve different comic versions of a story called "It Was a Dark and Silly Night." Readers will enjoy the different variations and the opportunity to write stories of their own. A compare-the-pictures game adds to the fun. This great book will appeal to a variety of readers. There are two other books in the series: *Strange Stories for Strange Kids* and *Little Lit: Folklore and Fairy Tale Funnies*.

More-Complex Picture Books

285   Gaiman, Neil. *The Day I Swapped My Dad for Two Goldfish.*

Ill. by Dave McKean. HarperCollins, 2004, ISBN 978-0-06-058701-7. 64p. ▪ **Grades 4–6**

A boy trades his dad for two goldfish, even though his little sister warns him he'll get in trouble. When Mom comes home, sure enough, he's in trouble. And when the boy goes to swap back his father, he finds himself caught in a whole series of trades.

286   Gaiman, Neil. *The Wolves in the Walls.*

Ill. by Dave McKean. HarperCollins, 2003, ISBN 978-0-380-97827-4. 56p. ▪ **Grades 4–6**

Lucy hears noises coming from the walls. When it turns out that there are wolves in the walls, her family leaves the house in fear. But it's Lucy and her pig puppet who are brave enough to save the day. The darker illustrations make this a scarier book, but one that will appeal to many readers. Older readers who like this style will also enjoy Gaiman's *Mr. Punch*.

287   Grey, Mini. *Traction Man Meets Turbo Dog.*

Ill. by author. Knopf, 2008, ISBN 978-0-375-85583-2. 32p. ▪ **Grades 2–3**

Traction Man returns in this adventure with Turbo Dog! Fans of the first Traction Man book will be excited to see the new adventures of Traction Man. The comic book-type illustrations mixed with a traditional picture-book format will engage male readers.

Partial Graphic Novels

288   Ehrenhaft, Daniel. *Drawing a Blank: Or How I Tried to Solve a Mystery, End a Feud, and Land the Girl of My Dreams.*

Ill. by Trevor Ristow. HarperCollins, 2006, ISBN 978-0-06-075252-1. 327p. ▪ **Grades 9–11**

When teenager Carlton Dunne's father is kidnapped, Carlton "escapes" from his boarding school and sets off to Scotland to try to rescue him. Adventures abound as he meets the mysterious girl of his dreams. Caught in an ancient feud, Carlton tries his best to save the day. Carlton is also a cartoonist, and the story contains samples of his work that mirror the story. A great young adult book interspersed with comics.

289   Primavera, Elise. *Fred and Anthony Escape from the Netherworld.*

Ill. by author. Hyperion, 2007, ISBN 978-0-7868-3677-2. 122p. ▪ Grades 2–4

Fred and Anthony love eating junk food and watching scary movies. They also hate to do homework, preferring to pay someone to do it for them. In this adventure, they find themselves in the Netherworld and must escape to save their lives. This fast-paced combination novel, comic book, and graphic novel will appeal even to reluctant readers. Part of a new series.

290   Primavera, Elise. *Fred and Anthony Meet the Demented Super-Degerm-O Zombie.*

Ill. by author. Hyperion, 2007, ISBN 978-0-7868-3679-6. 128p. ▪ Grades 2–4

Fred and Anthony are back, and they're still not crazy about doing homework. This is what lands them in trouble when they encounter the demented super-degerm-o zombie! Another trip to the Netherworld is in store for the boys. Readers will again enjoy the author's creative format.

291   Selznick, Brian. *The Invention of Hugo Cabret.*

Ill. by author. Scholastic, 2007, ISBN 978-0-439-81378-5. 544p. ▪ Grades 4–6
✪ Caldecott Medal

An absolutely amazing book! Don't let the number of pages fool your male readers. This story of the orphan Hugo who lives in a train station is told through both pictures and words. Selznick's illustrations will dazzle readers as they discover Hugo's secret mechanical man. Hugo learns more about the history of the invention and more about his father and the cinema as well. This Caldecott winner will fascinate readers for hours.

292   Wood, Don. *Into the Volcano.*

Ill. by author. Blue Sky Press, 2008, 978-0-439-72671-9. 176p. ▪ Grades 4–6

Sumno and Duffy are brothers who go to visit an aunt they have never met. When they discover that their aunt is up to no good, they soon find themselves inside a volcano. The brothers must try to escape and save their lives. This fast adventure will have readers anxious to see what happens to Sumno and Duffy.

Graphic Novels for Younger Readers

293   Colfer, Eoin, and Andrew Donkin, adapts. *Artemis Fowl: The Graphic Novel.*

Ill. by Giovanni Rigano and Paolo Lamanna. Hyperion, 2007 pap., ISBN 978-0-7868-4882-9. 112p. ▪ **Grades 4–6**

This is the graphic novel of *Artemis Fowl* (see entry 160). The story lends itself well to a graphic format and this version remains true to the original. Artemis concocts a scheme to kidnap one of the "fairy folk" in hopes of collecting ransom and starts a war between his world and the fairy world.

294   Horowitz, Anthony; adapt. by Antony Johnston. *Stormbreaker: The Graphic Novel.*

Ill. by Kanako Damerum and Yuzuru Takasaki. Philomel, 2006 pap., ISBN 978-0-399-24633-3. 144p. ▪ **Grades 5–7**

Alex Rider is back, now in a graphic novel. When Alex learns that the uncle he has been living with has died — and that he was a spy — he's shocked. But soon he too enters into the world of espionage, becoming a normal schoolboy by day and a secret spy the rest of the time. Readers will love the art combined with the action-packed adventure. There are many other Alex Rider books in conventional format.

295   Marunas, Nathaniel. *Manga Claus: The Blade of Kringle.*

Ill. by Erik Craddock. Razorbill, 2006, ISBN 978-1-59514-134-7. 80p. ▪ **Grades 2–3**

An unhappy elf wreaks havoc at the North Pole just before Santa is set to deliver the toys. Readers are taken on a tour of Santa's workshop and see a darker side of one of the elves. A graphic novel for younger readers.

296 Pyle, Kevin. *Blindspot.*

Holt, 2007 pap., ISBN 978-0-8050-7998-2. 96p.
- Grades 4–6

Dean is an eleven-year-old boy who lives near a forest — the perfect place for planning elaborate war games with his friends. When the boys' plan involves destroying an old shack, the game turns real, and people's lives are affected by the boys' actions.

297 Scieszka, Jon; adapt. by Zachary Rau. *Time Warp Trio: Nightmare on Joe's Street.*

HarperTrophy, 2006 pap., ISBN 978-0-06-111639-1. 96p.
- Grades 3–5

Further adventures of the Time Warp Trio, in graphic-novel format. In this book, the boys meet Frankenstein's monster! The only way to save the day and get back home is to find Mary Shelley, the author of *Frankenstein*. This graphic novel — based on the TV version of a popular series — will appeal to many boy readers.

298 Scieszka, Jon; adapt. by Zachary Rau. *Time Warp Trio: The Seven Blunders of the World.*

HarperTrophy, 2006 pap., ISBN 978-0-06-111637-7. 96p.
- Grades 3–5

Fans of the original books will love seeing their favorite characters in this format. The boys travel to ancient Babylon in this installment, and must find the book that helps them return to the present.

299 Smith, Jeff. *Bone: The Great Cow Race.*

Ill. by Steve Hamaker. Graphix, 2005, ISBN 978-0-439-70624-7. 136p. Series: Bone. - Grades 4–6

This is the second book in the Bone series. Fone Bone and his cousins are banished from Boneville. They must try to get back to their village. Sneaky cousin Phoney Bone gets people to bet on a race with a "mystery cow." This series and its hero, Fone Bone, have many fans. Other volumes include *Out From Boneville*, *Eyes of the Storm*, and *The Dragonslayer*.

300   Varon, Sarah. *Robot Dreams.*

Ill. by author. First Second, 2007 pap., ISBN 978-1-59643-108-9. 208p. ▪ **Grades 3–12**

In this nearly wordless graphic novel, Dog wants a friend. When a box with a robot in it arrives the next day Dog's wish has come true. He puts the robot together, and they have many fine adventures. However, one trip to the beach leaves Robot rusted. This causes a problem for their relationship as changes evolve for Robot.

Graphic Novels for Young Adults

301   Eisner, Will. *A Contract with God: And Other Tenement Stories.*

Ill. by author. DC Comics, 1996 pap., ISBN 978-1-56389-674-3. 184p. ▪ **Grades 9–12**

Eisner is one of the first graphic novelists. This is a collection of four of his first stories. They take place in a New York City tenement building and deal with people's struggles there. Readers will be fascinated by the ironies of life in the building.

302   Eisner, Will. *Will Eisner's New York: The Big City.*

Ill. by author. DC Comics, 1986 pap., ISBN 978-1-56389-682-8. 137p. ▪ **Grades 9–12**

The reader sees many different perspectives of life in New York, from people walking the sidewalks, window-watching, and front-stoop sitting. There are funny, sad, and puzzling anecdotes throughout the book.

303   Gipi. *Garage Band.*

Ill. by author. First Second, 2007 pap., ISBN 978-1-59643-206-2. 128p. ▪ **Grades 8–12**

In this graphic novel a young teen's father allows his son and his friends to have band practice in the garage, provided they stay out of trouble. Each boy has a checkered past, and this proves challenging when an amplifier blows up and they need new equipment. Decisions must be made when they learn they could steal one from a local church. Gipi has another graphic novel entitled *Notes for a War Story*.

304 Moore, Alan. *Watchmen.*
Ill. by Dave Gibbons. DC Comics, 1987 pap., ISBN 978-0-930289-23-2. 413p. ▪ **Grades 9–12**
❂ **Hugo Award**

This story is about a group of crime fighters called the Crimebusters. Years after their glory days, someone is trying to kill them one by one. This fast-paced graphic novel has garnered critical acclaim. Readers will enjoy the art and the mystery. Both authors have written other graphic novels.

305 Sacco, Joe. *Palestine.*
Ill. by author. Fantagraphics, 2002 pap., ISBN 978-1-56097-432-0. 296p. ▪ **Grades 9–12**

What was once a nine-issue comic series has been compiled into one book. It tells, in "comics journalism," the story of the author's two-month visit to Palestine in 1991–1992.

306 Sacco, Joe. *Safe Area Goražde: The War in Eastern Bosnia 1992–95.*
Ill. by author. Fantagraphics, 2000, ISBN 978-1-56097-392-8. 240p. ▪ **Grades 9 and up**

During the Bosnian War the author visited the "safe area" of Goražde four times. This is the story of his time there and of the people he met. He documents their struggle to come to terms with the war and its consequences.

307 Tan, Shaun. *The Arrival.*
Ill. by author. Arthur A. Levine, 2007, ISBN 978-0-439-89529-3. 128p. ▪ **Grades 6 and up**

This wordless graphic novel depicts a man's immigration to a new country. He has many struggles along the way, but forges a friendship and is able to communicate in a new language while discovering the new world around him. Readers will be intrigued by the incredible illustrations and the way they tell a story using no words. Tan has also written *The Lost Thing* (2004).

308 **Willingham, Bill. *Fables Vol. 2: Animal Farm.***
Ill. by Mark Buckingham and Steve Leialoha. Vertigo, 2003
pap., ISBN 978-1-4012-0077-0. 112p. ■ **Grades 9–12**

This installment in a series about fairy-tale characters living their
lives among everyday people is a twist on Orwell's *Animal Farm.*
This is definitely for older readers, and comparing it to the original
Animal Farm would make for an interesting discussion. Be aware
that some books in the series contain sexual or violent themes and
images. Other books in the 10-volume series include *The (Nearly)
Great Escape, Sons of Empire, The Mean Seasons,* and *Homelands.*

Sources

Cary, Stephen (2004). *Going Graphic: Comics at Work in the Multilingual
Clasroom.* Heinemann.

Chapter 8

Nonfiction

Dinosaurs, bugs, gross things, and biographies are just a few of the topics in this chapter that will interest boy readers. This chapter is a cornucopia of titles, many of them connecting with other titles in this book. So capitalize on boys' interest in nonfiction and watch them grow as readers. This chapter is divided into four sections: General Nonfiction, Animals, History, and Biographies/Autobiographies.

General Nonfiction

309   Blackburn, Ken, and Jeff Lammers. *Kids' Paper Air Plane Book.*
Workman, 1996 pap., ISBN 978-0-7611-0478-0. 160p.
- Grades 2 and up

If a boy wants to know how to make paper airplanes, this is the book for him — it was written by the world-record holder for paper airplanes! With so many different planes to create, readers will be busy for days.

310   Branzei, Sylvia. *Grossology.*
Ill. by Jack Keely. Price Stern Sloan, 2002 pap., ISBN 978-0-8431-4914-2. 80p. ▪ **Grades 3–6**

If it's gross, it will be in here, and it will definitely appeal to boys! From farts to boogers, all gross bodily functions are covered. Readers will learn about biology and enjoy it at the same time.

311   Branzei, Sylvia. *Grossology and You.*
Ill. by Jack Keely. Price Stern Sloan, 2002 pap., ISBN 978-0-8431-7736-7. 80p. ▪ **Grades 3–6**

Gross is back, and this time it's personal. Readers will enjoy this catalog of grossness and find out exactly how *they* are gross. More sneeze-stopping fun. Other gross books by this author include *Hands-On Grossology* and *Animal Grossology*.

312   Carter, David, and James Diaz. *The Elements of Pop-Up: A Pop-Up Book for Aspiring Paper Engineers.*
Scholastic, 1999, ISBN 0-689-82224-3. 18p. ▪ **Grades 4–7**

This is a book for anyone who loves pop-up books and would like to try to make one himself. There are examples of different types of pop-ups and step-by-step directions for making them. The designs highlighted by stars are great for beginners.

313   Cheney, Lynne. *Our 50 States: A Family Adventure Across America.*
Ill. by Robin Preiss Glasser. Simon & Schuster, 2006, ISBN 978-0-689-86717-0. 74p. ▪ **Grades 4–6**

This book takes the reader on a journey through all fifty states. Each page provides a plethora of information about the state. At times this can be overwhelming, but the reader can choose what to read and what to skip.

314   Cline-Ransome, Lesa. *Satchel Paige.*
Ill. by James Ransome. Simon & Schuster, 2000, ISBN 978-0-689-81151-7. 40p. ▪ **Grades 3–5**

This picture-book biography chronicles the life of the great pitcher from his troubled youth to his career in professional baseball. Life was never easy for Paige and this account highlights the struggles he endured. Amazing illustrations accompany the text. Try pairing this with *Satch and Me* (see entry 135).

315   Davies, Nicola. *Poop: A Natural History of the Unmentionable.*
Ill. by Neal Layton. Candlewick, 2004, ISBN 978-0-7636-3437-8. 61p. ▪ Grades 3–5
✪ Bulletin of the Center for Children's Books Blue Ribbon Nonfiction Book Award

Similar to Susan Goodman's poop book, this title covers types of animal poop (from sloppy to ploppy), the history of toilets, and the uses of poop. Cartoonish illustrations add humor.

316   Farrell, Jeanette. *Invisible Allies: Microbes That Shape Our Lives.*
Farrar, Straus & Giroux, 2005, ISBN 978-0-374-33608-0. 176p. ▪ Grades 6–9
✪ Bulletin of the Center for Children's Books Blue Ribbon Nonfiction Book Award

In this sequel to *Invisible Enemies* the author describes the many benefits of different microbes. Chapters including "Microbes at the Table," "Microbes Are Us," and "Rot Away" explain some of the positive functions of microbes, from food production to digestion.

317   Giblin, James Cross. *When Plague Strikes: The Black Death, Smallpox, AIDS.*
Ill. by David Frampton. HarperCollins, 1995, ISBN 978-0-06-025854-2. 212p. ▪ Grades 8 and up

The author compares the bubonic plague to epidemics of smallpox and AIDS. Similarities and differences in the treatment of these diseases are covered. This could be paired with Jim Murphy's *An American Plague* (see entry 351).

318   Goodman, Susan E. *Gee Whiz! It's All About Pee.*
Ill. by Elwood H. Smith. Viking, 2006, ISBN 978-0-670-06064-1. 40p. ▪ Grades 3–5

This title may gross out adults, which is why it's sure to please children, especially boys. The chapter titles ("Pees in a (Space) Pod," "War and Pees," and so on) bring humor to the topic. Information on "peeing through history," the scientific process of peeing, and the uses and function of urine is included.

319   Goodman, Susan E. *The Truth About Poop.*
Ill. by Elwood H. Smith. Viking, 2004, ISBN 978-0-670-03674-5. 40p. ■ **Grades 3–5**

How can boys not be attracted to a book like this? Chapters explain how different animals and humans poop. Of course, the history of the toilet is included. Finally the book covers the uses of poop. Playful illustrations accompany the fascinating facts.

320   Iggulden, Conn, and Hal Iggulden. *The Dangerous Book for Boys.*
HarperCollins, 2007, ISBN 978-0-06-124358-5. 288p.
■ **Grades 4–8**

If something appeals to boys, it will be in this handbook. It covers all the old-fashioned things boys enjoy doing, including coin tricks, camping, tying knots, and folding paper airplanes. Every boy will find something to enjoy in this all-inclusive book, which is available in versions for other countries including Great Britain and Australia.

321   Jackson, Donna M. *The Bug Scientists.*
Houghton Mifflin, 2002, ISBN 978-0-618-10868-8. 48p.
Series: Scientists in the Field. ■ **Grades 3–5**

Meet three bug scientists. From studying the ant world to crime-fighting insect investigation, those who study bugs have fascinating jobs. Readers will enjoy the photographs that accompany the text. Some of the other books in the Scientists in the Field series are *The Tarantula Scientist* (see entry 337), *Digging for Bird Dinosaurs*, *The Woods Scientist*, *The Wildlife Detectives*, and *Hidden Worlds*.

322   Jenkins, Steve. *The Top of the World: Climbing Mount Everest.*
Houghton Mifflin, 1999, ISBN 978-0-395-94218-5. 32p.
■ **Grades 3–5**

Jenkins takes the reader on a picture-book journey to the top of Mount Everest. He shows the reader everything he or she would need for trip. He also provides history about the mountain and those who have climbed it. The cut-paper illustrations are simply amazing and complement the text. This would pair well with Gordon Korman's Everest series (see entry 109) and Roland Smith's *Peak* (see entry 120).

323   McCloud, Scott. *Making Comics: Storytelling Secrets of Comics, Manga, and Graphic Novels.*
HarperPerennial, 2006 pap., ISBN 978-0-06-078094-4. 264p.
- Grades 6 and up

This could be the ultimate guide for aspiring cartoonists. Its focus is how to use different techniques to tell stories. Readers will see similarities between conventional books and the ways in which comics, manga, and graphic novels tell stories. In comic-book format, naturally. This is the third book in a great series.

324   McCloud, Scott. *Reinventing Comics: How Imagination and Technology Are Revolutionizing an Art Form.*
HarperPerennial, 2000 pap., ISBN 978-0-06-095350-8. 242p.
- Grades 6 and up

A companion to *Understanding Comics* (see below), this volume delves into the computer world and comics. Readers who enjoyed the first book, or who enjoy comics in general, will be interested in McCloud's ideas.

325   McCloud, Scott. *Understanding Comics: The Invisible Art.*
HarperPerennial, 1994 pap., ISBN 978-0-06-097625-5. 216p.
- Grades 6 and up

McCloud writes all about comics, from defining what they are to discussing how to create them. Of course, the book itself is in a comic-book format. Boys will enjoy this defense of comics as a genuine art form.

326   Madden, John, and Bill Gutman. *John Madden's Heroes of Football: The Story of America's Game.*
Dutton, 2006, ISBN 978-0-525-47698-6. 80p. ▪ Grades 4–6

John Madden, TV commentator and former head coach of the Oakland Raiders, knows football. In this book, he covers the history of the game and how it has developed. He also talks about influential players and how they have affected the game. Football fans will enjoy this in-depth look at the game.

327   Muller, Eric. *While You're Waiting for Your Food to Come: Experiments and Tricks That Can Be Done at a Restaurant, the Dining Room Table, or Wherever Food Is Served* .
       Ill. by Eldon Doty. Orchard, 1999, ISBN 978-0-531-30199-9. 84p. ▪ Grades 3–5

More than thirty activities using food will keep readers busy while they wait for dinner. Many can be used as science experiments at school or at home, and all will come in handy at restaurants.

328   Skurzynski, Gloria. *Are We Alone? Scientists Search for Life in Space.*
       National Geographic, 2004, ISBN 978-0-7922-6967-0. 92p. ▪ Grades 4–6

Could aliens really exist? Scientists are keeping their eyes on outer space to find out. Learn how they're searching for alien life forms and which planets may have life on them.

329   Temple, Kathryn. *Drawing: The Only Drawing Book You'll Ever Need to Be the Artist You've Always Wanted to Be.*
       Lark Books, 2005, ISBN 978-1-5799-0587-3. 112p. **Series: Art for Kids.** ▪ Grades 4–7

This is a great introduction to drawing, with details of various techniques. Basic principles are presented in an appealing format.

Animals

330   Arnold, Caroline. *Pterosaurs: Rulers of the Skies in the Dinosaur Age.*
       Ill. by Laurie Caple. Clarion, 2004, ISBN 978-0-618-31354-9. 40p. ▪ Grades 3–5

Books about dinosaurs abound, so it's always nice to see a fresh approach. Arnold provides detailed information about these flying dinosaurs. The watercolor illustrations will help readers picture the prehistoric skies.

331   Clarke, Ginjer L. *Bug Out! The World's Creepiest, Crawliest Critters.*

Ill. by Pete Mueller. Penguin, 2007 pap., ISBN 978-0-448-44543-4. 48p. **Series: All Aboard Science Reader.**
- Grades 2–3

This easy-to-read book covers basic information about bugs and insects — both helpful and scary. Younger readers who are ready for chapter books will appreciate this book and other titles in the series.

332   Cowley, Joy. *Red-Eyed Tree Frog.*

Photographs by Nic Bishop. Scholastic, 1999, ISBN 978-0-590-87175-4. 32p. **Series: Scholastic Bookshelf.**
- Grades 2–3

This is a simple story about the night of a red-eyed tree frog. The text is easy to read, but it's the photographs of the frogs that really make this book come to life. A few pages at the end of the book provide more detailed information about the frog.

333   Facklam, Margery. *The Big Bug Book.*

Ill. by Paul Facklam. Little, Brown, 1994, ISBN 978-0-316-27389-3. 32p. ■ **Grades 3–4**

Each double-page spread in this book presents a different kind of big bug, from the praying mantis to the tarantula. Adults may be creeped out by the realistic, life-sized illustrations but boys will relish the information and pictures.

334   Jenkins, Steve. *What Do You Do When Something Wants to Eat You?*

Houghton Mifflin, 1997, ISBN 978-0-395-82514-3. 32p.
- Grades 3–4

Jenkins answers the title question. On each page he introduces an animal and the defense mechanism it uses. The intricate cut-paper illustrations help readers enjoy learning more about animals. Pair this with *What Do You Do with a Tail Like This?* (see entry 336).

335   Jenkins, Steve, and Robin Page. *I See a Kookaburra! Discovering Animal Habitats Around the World.*
Houghton Mifflin, 2005, ISBN 978-0-618-50764-1. 32p.
- Grades 2–4
- ✪ Bulletin of the Center for Children's Books Blue Ribbon Non-fiction Book Award

What do you see in the jungle? A tide pool? The forest? Find out which animals live in which habitats. The end of the book gives facts about each animal presented. Incredibly detailed illustrations add to the fun.

336   Jenkins, Steve, and Robin Page. *What Do You Do With a Tail Like This?*
Houghton Mifflin, 2003, ISBN 978-0-618-25628-0. 32p.
- Grades 2–3
- ✪ Caldecott Honor Book

Tails serve as clues to animal identities in this informative book. Other body parts are discussed too. The illustrations are absolutely fabulous and intricately detailed.

337   Montgomery, Sy. *The Tarantula Scientist.*
Photographs by Nic Bishop. Houghton Mifflin, 2004, ISBN 978-0-618-14799-1. 80p. Series: Scientists in the Field.
- Grades 4–6
- ✪ Robert F. Sibert Honor Book

Everything a reader wants to know about tarantulas: their habitats, diets, and more. Boys will love the cool photographs.

338   Siy, Alexandra, and Dennis Kunkel. *Mosquito Bite.*
Charlesbridge, 2005, ISBN 978-1-5709-1591-8. 32p.
- Grades 3–4

Everything you've ever wanted to know about these pesky blood-sucking creatures, with magnified illustrations to enhance the text and make you itch.

339   Tanaka, Shelley. *New Dinos: The Latest Finds! The Coolest Dinosaur Discoveries!*

Ill. by Alan Barnard. Atheneum, 2002, ISBN 978-0-689-85183-4. 48p. ▪ **Grades 3–5**

Dinosaurs are always popular, and this book about newly discovered dinosaurs (as of 2002) will fascinate readers. Readers learn where they were found, what they may have looked like, and even what their dung can tell us.

History

340   Bartoletti, Susan Campbell. *Hitler Youth: Growing Up in Hitler's Shadow.*

Scholastic, 2005, ISBN 978-0-439-35379-3. 176p.
▪ **Grades 5–9**
✪ **Newbery Honor Book, Robert F. Sibert Honor Book, Bulletin of the Center for Children's Books Blue Ribbon Nonfiction Book Award**

Bartoletti covers Hitler's rise to power and the influence of the organization called Hitler Youth. Individuals who were in the Hitler Youth — and those who resisted the group — tell their stories. This book provides fascinating and troubling information about the time period.

341   Calabro, Marian. *The Perilous Journey of the Donner Party.*

Clarion, 1999, ISBN 978-0-395-86610-8. 192p.
▪ **Grades 5–7**

Calabro describes the Donner Party's journey from Illinois to California. The trek is told through the eyes of a thirteen-year-old girl, whose letter is reproduced at the end of the book. Readers will be amazed by what occurred on the trip.

342   Crowe, Chris. *Getting Away with Murder: The True Story of the Emmett Till Case.*

Phyllis Fogelman Books, 2003, ISBN 978-0-8037-2804-2. 128p. ▪ **Grades 7–9**

✪ **Jane Addams Honor Book**

Emmett Till was a fourteen-year-old African American boy from Chicago. He was visiting his family in Mississippi when he allegedly whistled at a white woman. Three days later his badly beaten body was found. The book discusses the murder trial — which resulted in acquittal — and the events that followed it. Try pairing this with *Mississippi Trial: 1955*, also by Chris Crowe.

343   Denenberg, Barry. *Lincoln Shot! A President's Life Remembered.*

Ill. by Christopher Bing. Feiwel and Friends, 2008, ISBN 978-0-312-37013-8. 40p. ▪ **Grades 3–5**

This is a new biography of Lincoln in picture-book format. The illustrations use 19th-century newspaper style. This creative approach will draw readers into the story of Abraham Lincoln.

344   Freedman, Russell. *Kids at Work: Lewis Hine and the Crusade Against Child Labor.*

Clarion, 1994, ISBN 978-0-395-58703-4. 112p. ▪ **Grades 5–7**

Freedman uses authentic photographs by former teacher Lewis Hine to depict the outrageous working conditions of children, some as young as three, from 1908 to 1918. Freedman also wrote the Newbery-winning *Lincoln: A Photobiography*.

345   Freedman, Russell. *Who Was First? Discovering the Americas.*

Clarion, 2007, ISBN 978-0-618-66391-0. 96p. ▪ **Grades 4–7**

This book examines the question of who really did discover America. While millions of schoolchildren have learned that it was Columbus, Freedman provides new evidence that it could have been a number of other people. Readers will enjoy the new information about America's discovery.

346   Harness, Cheryl. *Ghosts of the Nile.*

Simon & Schuster, 2004, ISBN 978-0-689-83478-3. 32p.
- Grades 3–5

A boy is exploring the Egyptian section of a museum when he suddenly finds himself getting a much more in-depth tour than expected. He learns firsthand about ancient Egyptian culture, the pyramids, and the Nile river. Each page is packed with information. Another book in the series is *Ghosts of the Civil War*.

347   Harness, Cheryl. *Ghosts of the White House.*

Simon & Schuster, 1998, ISBN 0-689-80872-0. 48p.
- Grades 3–5

Sara gets an unanticipated tour of the White House when expired presidents tell her about the history behind its rooms. Sidebars give details on each of the presidents. Packed with information about American history.

348   Hoose, Phillip. *We Were There, Too! Young People in U.S. History.*

Farrar, Straus & Giroux, 2001, ISBN 978-0-374-38252-0. 276p. - Grades 4–6

Hoose finally gives children credit for what they have done to influence U.S. history. From the young boy who sailed with Columbus to a boy who pitched for the Cincinnati Reds during World War II, children who were there have their stories told. Try pairing this with Hoose's other title, *It's Our World, Too!*

349   Levine, Ellen. *Darkness Over Denmark: The Danish Resistance and the Rescue of the Jews.*

Holiday House, 2000, ISBN 978-0-8234-1447-5. 164p.
- Grades 5–8

The Danish effort to smuggle Jews into Sweden during World War II is described by survivors. This book would be well paired with Lois Lowry's *Number the Stars* or Susan Campbell Bartoletti's *Hitler Youth*.

350   **Martin, Bill, Jr., and Michael Sampson.** *I Pledge Allegiance.*

Ill. by Chris Raschka. Candlewick, 2002, ISBN 978-0-7636-1648-9. 32p. ■ **Grades 2–4**

Each double-page spread in this book presents a few words from the Pledge of Allegiance. Side text defines vocabulary words and explains the history of the pledge and of the United States.

351   **Murphy, Jim.** *An American Plague: The True and Terrifying Story of the Yellow Fever Epidemic of 1793.*

Clarion, 2003, ISBN 978-0-395-77608-7. 176p.
■ **Grades 5–7**
✪ **Newbery Honor Book, Robert F. Sibert Medal**

Murphy discusses how the outbreak started, what finally ended it, and how it devastated the population of Philadelphia. Readers may feel a little ill when they finish this book. Pair it with Laurie Halse Anderson's *Fever 1793* for great discussions.

352   **Murphy, Jim.** *Blizzard!*

Scholastic, 2000, ISBN 978-0-590-67309-9. 136p.
■ **Grades 5–7**

This time Murphy takes on the blizzard that hammered the East Coast for three days in 1888 . Survivor accounts will make the storm seem real to readers. Be warned: This book will give you a chill!

353   **Murphy, Jim.** *Gone A-Whaling: The Lure of the Sea and the Hunt for the Great Whale.*

Clarion, 1998, ISBN 978-0-395-69847-1. 208p.
■ **Grades 6–9**

Jump on board a whaling ship for an adventure. Find out what it's like to work on the ship, how to use the tools of the trade, and what it takes to hunt these huge sea creatures. Fans of this book will like Murphy's other titles: *Inside the Alamo*, *The Great Fire*, *Blizzard!*, and *An American Plague*.

354   Murphy, Jim. *The Great Fire.*

Scholastic, 1995, ISBN 978-0-590-47267-8. 144p.
- Grades 5–7
- Newbery Honor Book

Murphy's in-depth focus for this book is the citywide fire that devastated Chicago in 1871. He covers how the fire may have started, the disaster it created, and the rebuilding of the city. Readers will be fascinated.

355   Murphy, Jim. *Inside the Alamo.*

Delacorte, 2003, ISBN 978-0-385-32574-5. 122p.
- Grades 5–7

Murphy takes the reader into the confrontation at the Alamo. Separating fact from fiction, he addresses the great battle and the preparation for it. The book also covers the key people in the struggle and gives readers insights into the times.

356   Nelson, Kadir. *We Are the Ship: The Story of Negro League Baseball.*

Jump at the Sun, 2008, ISBN 978-0-7868-0832-8. 96p.
- Grades 4–6

Nelson tells the story of the Negro baseball leagues. He provides anecdotes from history about players, owners, games, and other adventures of what it was like to be around during this era. The information, accompanied by absolutely amazing illustrations, will have readers intrigued to learn more about the league and its players. Could be the Caldecott winner for 2009?

357   Parry, Richard. *Trial by Ice: The True Story of Murder and Survival on the 1871 Polaris Expedition.*

Ballantine, 2001, ISBN 978-0-345-43925-3. 336p.
- Grades 9–12

Parry tells of the doomed 1871 *Polaris* expedition to the North Pole. The murder of Captain Hall and the crew's fight to survive will intrigue young adult readers.

358   St. George, Judith. *So You Want to Be an Inventor?*

Ill. by David Small. Philomel, 2002, ISBN 978-0-399-23593-1. 48p. ▪ **Grades 3–5**

This sequel is for everyone who enjoyed *So You Want to Be President?* (see below). The same format is used, but the subject is inventors through history. A variety of inventors, their inventions, how they came up with their ideas, and additional quirky information are all covered. Another book in the series is *So You Want to Be an Explorer?*

359   St. George, Judith. *So You Want to Be President?*

Ill. by David Small. Philomel, 2000, ISBN 978-0-399-23407-1. 48p. ▪ **Grades 3–5**
✪ **Caldecott Medal**

Interesting facts about all the U.S. presidents, including their shapes, sizes, talents, families, and interests. The cartoon-like illustrations add to the appeal and will help readers become experts on the presidents.

360   Tanaka, Shelley. *Secrets of the Mummies.*

Ill. by Greg Ruhl. Hyperion, 1999, ISBN 978-0-7868-0473-3. 48p. Series: I Was There. ▪ **Grades 3–5**

Curious readers will discover the secrets of mummification and see photographs of mummies. Readers will be fascinated by the text as well as the photographs and illustrations.

361   Yolen, Jane, and Heidi Elisabet Yolen Stemple. *The Salem Witch Trials: An Unsolved Mystery from History.*

Ill. by Roger Roth. Simon & Schuster, 2004, ISBN 978-0-689-84620-5. 32p. Series: Unsolved Mystery from History. ▪ **Grades 3–4**

Readers can look for clues into what started the hysteria in Salem, Massachusetts, in 1692. The book tells the story of the witch hunts, provides historical information, and defines key vocabulary. Other books in the series are *Roanoke: the Lost Colony*, *The Mary Celeste*, and *The Wolf Girls*.

Biographies/Autobiographies

362   Blumberg, Rhoda. *Shipwrecked! The True Adventures of a Japanese Boy.*

HarperCollins, 2001, ISBN 978-0-688-17484-2. 80p.
- Grades 5–7

In 1841, fourteen-year-old Manjirō was shipwrecked on an island 300 miles from shore, wondering if he would ever return to Japan. Manjirō became the first Japanese person to set foot in America, and his experiences here fascinated his countrymen.

363   Brown, Don. *Odd Boy Out: Young Albert Einstein.*

Houghton Mifflin, 2004, ISBN 978-0-618-49298-5. 32p.
- Grades 3–4
- ✪ Bulletin of the Center for Children's Books Blue Ribbon Nonfiction Book Award

Boys who feel misunderstood at school will relate to this picture-book biography of Albert Einstein, who was a unique boy who had different interests from his schoolmates. The illustrations emphasize young Einstein's outsider status.

364   Crutcher, Chris. *King of the Mild Frontier: An Ill-Advised Autobiography.*

HarperCollins, 2003, ISBN 0-06-050249-5. 260p.
- Grades 7–9

Crutcher talks about his upbringing in Idaho and the somewhat tricky relationship he had with his parents. Readers will see connections between the author's life and his young adult novels, which include *Deadline*, *Staying Fat for Sarah Byrnes*, and *Whale Talk*.

365   Fleischman, John. *Phineas Gage: A Gruesome but True Story About Brain Science.*

Houghton Mifflin, 2002, ISBN 0-618-05252-6. 85p.
- Grades 4–6

Phineas Gage was a man who suffered a horrific head trauma in 1848. This book tells of his accident and how he was treated. It compares brain science then with what we know now. Readers will be enthralled by the gruesome story. With photographs.

366   Fleischman, Sid. *The Abracadabra Kid: A Writer's Life.*
Greenwillow, 1996, ISBN 978-0-688-14859-1. 208p.
- Grades 4–7

In this autobiography, Sid Fleischman reveals what led him to become a writer. His true passion is magic, and he talks of his time as a magician and his transformation into a writer.

367   Fleischman, Sid. *Escape! The Story of the Great Houdini.*
Greenwillow, 2006, ISBN 978-0-06-085094-4. 210p.
- Grades 4–6

There are many biographies about Houdini, but who better to write a new one than fellow magician Sid Fleischman? Fleischman covers the life of Houdini and tells an interesting story as well. He also has some tricks up his sleeve: never-before-seen pictures that were given to him by Houdini's wife. This is a great biography for anyone interested in magic or escape artists.

368   Gantos, Jack. *Hole in My Life.*
Farrar, Straus & Giroux, 2002, ISBN 978-0-374-39988-7. 200p. ■ Grades 6–9
❂ Robert F. Sibert Honor Book

In this autobiographical book Gantos (author of the Joey Pigza books) writes about a difficult period in his life. Just starting college and working a summer job, he's offered $10,000 to smuggle and sell drugs in New York City. Gantos describes the struggles he faced in prison after he was caught and how he began to write.

369   Herbert, Janis. *Marco Polo for Kids: His Marvelous Journey to China: 21 Activities.*
Chicago Review Press, 2001 pap., ISBN 1-5565-2377-7. 130p.
- Grades 5–7

This book follows the adventures of Marco Polo as he travels to China. Twenty-one activities relate to the cultures the explorer encountered on his journey. Readers can learn phrases in Turkish, make a mosaic, and put on a Chinese-style opera.

370   Kerley, Barbara. *The Dinosaurs of Waterhouse Hawkins.*

Ill. by Brian Selznick. Scholastic, 2001, ISBN 978-0-439-11494-3. 48p. ▪ **Grades 3–5**
✪ **Caldecott Honor Book**

This book chronicles the life of Waterhouse Hawkins, a scientist who loved to study dinosaurs. The book is divided into three "acts." The phenomenal illustrations add to the beautiful story.

371   Krull, Kathleen. *Leonardo da Vinci.*

Ill. by Boris Kulikov. Viking, 2005, ISBN 978-0-670-05920-1. 124p. **Series: Giants of Science.** ▪ **Grades 4–6**

Many people know of Leonardo da Vinci as a great artist. But he was also a scientist. He even conducted illegal human dissections! Readers will be intrigued by the new information they learn about the famous artist. Other books in the series include *Isaac Newton*, *Sigmund Freud*, and *Marie Curie*.

372   Krull, Kathleen. *Lives of the Athletes: Thrills, Spills (and What the Neighbors Thought).*

Ill. by Kathryn Hewitt. Harcourt, 1997, ISBN 0-15-200806-3. 96p. ▪ **Grades 4–6**

Each chapter about a famous athlete provides a short biography and some not-so-well-known facts. This is a fun book for readers who want to know more about many athletes from history.

373   Myers, Walter Dean. *Bad Boy: A Memoir.*

Amistad, 2001, ISBN 978-0-06-029523-3. 224p. ▪ **Grades 6–9**

In this autobiography, Myers talks of his childhood in Harlem, New York, and his lifelong love of reading, which he sometimes had to hide. During his teenage years Myers struggled with school and his desire to be a writer. Fans of his work will enjoy discovering what led him to become a writer. This book is a great way to hook reluctant readers and give them a role model.

374   Partridge, Elizabeth. *John Lennon: All I Want Is the Truth.*
Viking, 2005, ISBN 978-0-670-05954-6. 256p.
- Grades 9–12
- ✪ Bulletin of the Center for Children's Books Blue Ribbon Nonfiction Book Award

In this photographic biography, Partridge sets out to tell readers the true story of John Lennon and let them discover what he was really like. Using Lennon's own writings as well as numerous interviews, the author describes the person behind the music. A great biography for young adult readers.

375   Paulsen, Gary. *Guts: The True Stories Behind Hatchet and the Brian Books.*
Delacorte, 2001, ISBN 978-0-385-32650-6. 144p.
- Grades 4–6

Boys who have wondered about Brian's adventures of Brian in the Hatchet books will treasure this autobiography. Paulsen talks about the adventures he had growing up and how he wove them into *Hatchet*. Boys will be spellbound.

376   Paulsen, Gary. *How Angel Peterson Got His Name.*
Random House, 2003, ISBN 978-0-385-72949-9. 128p.
- Grades 5–8

Paulsen recollects funny stories from when he and his friends were thirteen-year-old boys. The boys try to wrestle a bear, snow-ski behind a car, shoot waterfalls in a barrel, and so much more. Boys will read with glee and wonder if they can improve on some of the ideas Paulsen and his friends tried.

377   Paulsen, Gary. *My Life in Dog Years.*
Delacorte, 1998, ISBN 978-0-385-32570-7. 144p.
- Grades 4–7

In this "autodogography," Paulsen talks about all of the dogs he has had, from his first dog as a boy to the sled dogs he raced in the Iditarod and his current companions. Fans of Paulsen's fiction will enjoy reading about his real-life adventures with the dogs. This book will make a great discussion-starter for boys who have also read *Guts*.

378   Scieszka, Jon. *Knucklehead.*

Penguin, 2008 forthcoming. ▪ **Grades 4–6**

Scieszka describes his childhood and his experiences both at school and at home with his family. Growing up with five brothers alone could provide some funny stories, but Scieszka sprinkles in some classic school stories too. Boys will love learning more about one of their favorite authors, and the cover alone will draw them into the book.

379   Sis, Peter. *The Wall: Growing Up Behind the Iron Curtain.*

Farrar, Straus & Giroux, 2007, ISBN 978-0-374-34701-7. 56p.
▪ **Grades 3–6**
✪ **Caldecott Honor Book**

Sis tells the story of his life growing up in Prague during the Cold War and the struggles he endured. He weaves his story through text and amazing illustrations. Readers will be dazzled by the artwork and struck by the challenges Sis faced.

380   Spinelli, Jerry. *Knots in My Yo-yo String: The Autobiography of a Kid.*

Knopf, 1998, ISBN 978-0-679-98791-8. 148p. ▪ **Grades 4–6**

Jerry Spinelli is a well-known children's author. In this autobiography, he spends a lot of time talking about his youth and his love of sports. Though he didn't want to become a writer when he was young, readers will be glad he did when they pick up this funny, dramatic, and wild adventure.

381   Winter, Jonah. *Roberto Clemente: Pride of the Pittsburgh Pirates.*

Ill. by Raúl Colón. Atheneum, 2005, ISBN 978-0-689-85643-3. 32p. ▪ **Grades 3–4**

This is a picture-book biography about Roberto Clemente, the famous baseball player from Puerto Rico. It begins with Clemente learning to play baseball as a child and covers his adult life as a professional player. Fabulous illustrations accompany the story.

Chapter 9

Modern Classics

For most chapters in this book, I have been careful to select titles that were published within the last ten years, although in some cases I made exceptions. Most of the books in this chapter were published more than ten years ago, but I couldn't resist including them. The bibliographic information refers to currently available editions; if it differs, the original date of publication is mentioned in the annotation. These books are favorites that boys will always enjoy reading, and I hope you will continue to recommend them as well. This chapter is divided into two sections: Picture Books and Novels.

Picture Books

382   Steig, William. *Dr. De Soto.*
Farrar, Straus & Giroux, 1990 pap., ISBN 978-0-374-41810-6.
32p. ▪ **Grades 2–4**

A great picture book about a dentist who also happens to be a mouse. When a fox comes to his office one day with a horrible toothache, Dr. De Soto knows he must be careful. He and his wife manage to outsmart the fox. First published in 1982, this book was followed by *Dr. DeSoto Goes to Africa* (1992).

Novels

383 **Alexander, Lloyd.** *The Black Cauldron.*
Holt, 2006 pap., ISBN 978-0-8050-8049-0. 208p. **Series: Prydain Chronicles.** ▪ **Grades 5–7**
✪ **Newbery Honor Book**

This is the second book in the Prydain Chronicles. It follows Taran, an assistant pig-keeper in Prydain, as he undertakes a quest to destroy the Black Cauldron, which is creating undead creatures that threaten the land of Prydain. First published in 1965.

384 **Anderson, Laurie Halse.** *Speak.*
Farrar, Straus & Giroux, 1999, ISBN 978-0-374-37152-4. 208p. ▪ **Grades 9–12**

During the summer before ninth grade, a horrible thing happens to Melinda at a party. She's so traumatized that she won't talk to anyone. The reader slowly finds out what happened as Melinda describes the monotony of high school. Anderson skillfully uses humor to help lighten the tone of a book that all young adults should read. This novel pairs well with Klass's *You Don't Know Me* (see entry 74).

385 **Brown, Jeff.** *Flat Stanley.*
Ill. by Scott Nash. Scholastic, 1974 pap., ISBN 978-0-590-04528-5. 65p. ▪ **Grades 2–3**

When a bulletin board falls on Stanley he's not hurt, just flattened. This book is the beginning of the series all about Stanley, who is only 14 millimeters thick. Young readers will enjoy Stanley's adventures. *Flat Stanley* was first published in 1964 with illustrations by Tomi Ungerer. Other books in the series include *Stanley, Flat Again!*; *Stanley in Space*; and *Invisible Stanley*.

386 **Cleary, Beverly.** *The Mouse and the Motorcycle.*
HarperTrophy, 2006 pap., ISBN 978-0-380-70924-3. 176p. ▪ **Grades 3–5**

Ralph is a mouse who gets to live his dream of adventure when a young boy lets him ride his toy motorcycle. Boys who love animals will especially enjoy this first book in the Ralph trilogy, which first appeared in 1965.

387   Fitzgerald, John D. *The Great Brain.*
Putnam, 2004 pap., ISBN 978-0-14-240058-6. 192p.
- Grades 4–6

John Fitzgerald's older brother Tom has a great brain. He's able to outsmart every child in his neighborhood, and sometimes the adults as well. Readers will need to pay close attention so they're not out-smarted too. First published in the 1960s, this series is set in Utah in the 1890s. Other books in the series include *More Adventures of the Great Brain*, *Me and My Little Brain*, *The Great Brain Reforms*, *Return of the Great Brain*, and *The Great Brain Is Back*.

388   Fleischman, Sid. *McBroom's Ghost.*
Ill. by Amy Wummer. Price Stern Sloan, 1998 pap., ISBN 978-0-8431-7948-4. 62p. **Series: The Adventures of McBroom.** - **Grades 2–3**

Josh McBroom is a farmer who tells some very tall tales. Readers should pay close attention so they won't be fooled. Other books in the series include *McBroom Tells a Lie*, *McBroom Tells the Truth* (a graphic novel), and *Here Comes McBroom*. This book was first published in 1971 with illustrations by Robert Frankenberg.

389   Fleischman, Sid. *Mr. Mysterious and Company.*
Ill. by Eric Von Schmidt. HarperTrophy, 1997 pap., ISBN 978-0-688-14922-2. 160p. - Grades 4–6

The Hacketts are traveling magicians who cross the Wild West in a wagon putting on magic shows. Their goal is to reach California so that Pa can retire. Each performance along their route results in hilarity. Originally published in 1962.

390   Korman, Gordon. *No Coins, Please.*
Apple, 1991 pap., ISBN 978-0-590-44208-4. 192p.
- Grades 4–6

Artie Gellar is an eleven-year-old who just happens to be the world's greatest entrepreneur. When his mom signs him up for a cross-country tour she warns the counselors to keep an eye on him. But at each stop Artie is off concocting a moneymaking scheme. Each one is more elaborate than the one before, leading to the ultimate scheme in Las Vegas. This one is my all-time favorite children's book. It was first published in 1984.

391   Korman, Gordon. *This Can't Be Happening at MacDonald Hall.*
Scholastic, 1996 pap., ISBN 978-0-590-44213-8. 118p.
- Grades 4–6

Bruno and Boots attend (and in their minds, run) a boarding school in Canada. The boys keep busy contending with teachers, the head-master, and their friends at the all-girls school across the road. Kor-man wrote this first book in the series when he was in seventh grade. Other books in the series include *Something Fishy at MacDonald Hall*, *The War With Mr. Wizzle*, *Zucchini Warriors*, and *MacDonald Hall Goes Hollywood*. *This Can't Be Happening at MacDonald Hall* was first published in 1978.

392   Le Guin, Ursula K. *A Wizard of Earthsea.*
Spectra, 2004 pap., ISBN 978-0-553-38304-1. 192p. **Series: The Earthsea Cycle.** - Grades 5–7

A young boy called Sparrowhawk takes a perilous journey to become a wizard. When Sparrowhawk graduates from school and becomes a young man, he must face a serious mistake he made as a student. In this first book in the dark fantasy series readers will see similarities to the Harry Potter series. *A Wizard of Earthsea* was first published in 1968.

393   L'Engle, Madeleine. *A Wrinkle in Time.*
Square Fish, 2007 pap., ISBN 978-0-312-36754-1. 224p.
- Grades 5–7
- ✪ Newbery Medal

Meg Murry is sent on a quest to find her father. Her brother Charles Wallace and friend Calvin join her and they travel through time and space on a "wrinkle in time," or tesseract. This is a great series that will engage readers who love science fiction. *A Wrinkle in Time* first appeared in 1962.

394 **Lewis, C. S.** *The Lion, the Witch and the Wardrobe.*
HarperCollins, 2005 pap., ISBN 978-0-06-076489-0. 256p.
- Grades 5–7

Four siblings step through a wardrobe into a frozen land called Narnia, where they are caught in the middle of a battle between good and evil. The epic struggle even pits the siblings against one another. Lewis's classic Chronicles of Narnia series continues to engage readers, especially after being made into a movie. *The Lion, the Witch and the Wardrobe* was first published in 1950.

395 **Manes, Stephen.** *Be a Perfect Person in Just Three Days!*
Ill. by Thomas Huffman. Yearling, 1998 pap., ISBN 978-0-440-22790-8. 96p. - Grades 3–5

Milo is far from perfect, and he can't stand it. One day he is hit on the head in the library — by a book called *Be a Perfect Person in Just Three Days!* The author, Dr. K. Pinkerton Silverfish, seems nice enough. So Milo begins a three-day quest to be perfect. *Be a Perfect Person in Just Three Days!* first appeared in 1982.

396 **Manes, Stephen.** *Make Four Million Dollars by Next Thursday!*
Yearling, 1991 pap., ISBN 978-0-440-41370-7. 96p.
- Grades 3–5

Jason Nozzle has no pocket money, but he does have a muddy book that promises to make him rich. Following the instructions of the author, Dr. K. Pinkerton Silverfish, Jason sets out to become rich by next Thursday.

397 **Paulsen, Gary.** *Harris and Me.*
Harcourt, 2007, ISBN 978-0-15-292877-3. 168p.
- Grades 5–8

The eleven-year-old narrator is dropped off at the home of his nine-year-old cousin, Harris. Harris immediately asks if his parents really are "puke drunks." Thus begins a wild summer when wrestling pigs and peeing on electric fences are only the highlights. A zany story for upper-elementary and middle-school readers, this was first published in 1993.

398   **Sobol, Donald J.** *Encyclopedia Brown: Boy Detective.*
Putnam, 2007 pap., ISBN 978-0-14-240888-9. 96p.
- Grades 3–5

Leroy "Encyclopedia" Brown is a ten-year-old star detective, helping children in his town solve mysteries and settle disputes. His father happens to be the town's police chief, so at the dinner table each night Encyclopedia hears about the latest cases and helps his father fight crime. Each book in this series contains ten mysteries. Other books in the series include *Encyclopedia Brown and the Case of the Secret Pitch*, *Encyclopedia Brown Finds the Clues*, and *Encyclopedia Brown Gets His Man*. *Encyclopedia Brown: Boy Detective* first appeared in print in 1963.

399   **Soto, Gary.** *Baseball in April and Other Stories.*
Harcourt, 2000 pap., ISBN 978-0-15-202567-0. 128p.
- Grades 5–7

Eleven different short stories feature young people, mostly Latinos, growing up in central California. Sports, the opposite sex, and family are some of the themes. Spanish words are mixed in throughout and there is a glossary at the end. First published in 1990.

400   **Soto, Gary.** *The Pool Party.*
Delacorte, 1993, ISBN 978-0-385-30890-8. 104p.
- Grades 4–6

Rudy is a regular boy from a Hispanic family. He's thrown for a loop when a rich girl in his class invites him to a pool party. After many admonitions from his family he heads to the party and celebrates the girl's birthday in her family's pool. Soto mixes in Spanish words and phrases throughout the book. A glossary is provided.

401   **Speare, Elizabeth George.** *The Sign of the Beaver.*
Dell, 1993 pap., ISBN 978-0-440-77903-2. 160p. - Grades 4–6
✪ Newbery Honor Book

In the late 1700s, twelve-year-old Matt must survive on his own in the wilderness when his father leaves their homestead to retrieve his mother and sister. When Matt is stung by a swarm of bees he's rescued by Native Americans who nurse him back to health. The chief of the tribe befriends him and asks Matt to teach his grandson to read and write. First published in 1984.

Author Index

References are to entry numbers, not page numbers.
Illustrator names are listed in parentheses.

E

F

Title Index

Titles (in italics) are followed by the name of the principal author, series title if applicable, and entry number.

L

M

T

U

V

W

Subject Index

References are to entry numbers, not page numbers.
Grade levels follow entry numbers.

159

Adventure — Fiction (cont.)

Hiaasen, Carl
Flush, 102 [5–7]
Hobbs, Will
Crossing the Wire, 103 [5–8]
Far North, 104 [5–8]
Leaving Protection, 105 [6–9]
River Thunder, 106 [6–9]
Wild Man Island, 107 [5–8]
Horowitz, Anthony
Stormbreaker: The Graphic Novel, 294 [5–7]
Karr, Kathleen
The Great Turkey Walk, 222 [4–6]
Korman, Gordon
Chasing the Falconers, 108 [4–6]
The Contest, 109 [4–6]
The Discovery, 110 [4–6]
Kidnapped: The Abduction, 111 [4–6]
Shipwreck, 112 [4–6]
Landy, Derek
Skullduggery Pleasant, 174 [4–7]
Le Guin, Ursula K.
A Wizard of Earthsea, 392 [5–7]
L'Engle, Madeleine
A Wrinkle in Time, 393 [5–7]
Lethcoe, Jason
The Misadventures of Benjamin Bartholomew Piff: You Wish, 175 [3–5]
Lewis, C. S.
The Lion, the Witch and the Wardrobe, 394 [5–7]
Marunas, Nathaniel
Manga Claus: The Blade of Kringle, 295 [2–3]
Paulsen, Gary
Brian's Hunt, 113 [5–7]
Brian's Return, 114 [5–7]
Brian's Winter, 115 [5–7]
Call Me Francis Tucket, 228 [4–6]
Hatchet, 116 [4–6]
Mr. Tucket, 229 [4–6]
Tucket's Gold, 230 [4–6]
Pearson, Ridley, and Dave Barry
Peter and the Starcatchers, 181 [5–8]

Philbrick, Rodman
The Young Man and the Sea, 117 [5–8]
Pyle, Kevin
Blindspot, 296 [4–6]
Scieszka, Jon
Time Warp Trio: Nightmare on Joe's Street, 297 [3–5]
Time Warp Trio: The Seven Blunders of the World, 298 [3–5]
Smelcer, John
The Trap, 118 [5–7]
Smith, Jeff
Bone: The Great Cow Race, 299 [4–6]
Smith, Roland
Jack's Run, 119 [6 and up]
Peak, 120 [6 and up]
Snicket, Lemony
The Bad Beginning, 121 [4–6]
Soto, Gary
Crazy Weekend, 91 [4–6]
Speare, Elizabeth George
The Sign of the Beaver, 401 [4–6]
Wood, Don
Into the Volcano, 292 [4–6]

African Americans

Nelson, Kadir
We Are the Ship: The Story of Negro League Baseball, 356 [4–6]

African Americans — Biography

Cline-Ransome, Lesa
Satchel Paige, 314 [3–5]
Myers, Walter Dean
Bad Boy: A Memoir, 373 [6–9]

African Americans — Fiction

Coy, John
Strong to the Hoop, 125 [3–5]
Curtis, Christopher Paul
Bud, Not Buddy, 210 [4–6]
Elijah of Buxton, 211 [4–6]
The Watsons Go to Birmingham — 1963, 212 [4–6]
Grimes, Nikki
Bronx Masquerade, 70 [8–11]

Cold War — Biography
Sis, Peter
> *The Wall: Growing Up Behind the Iron Curtain,* 379 [3–6]

Columbus, Christopher — Fiction
Yolen, Jane
> *Encounter,* 201 [3–5]

Concrete poetry
Janeczko, Paul
> *A Poke in the Eye: A Collection of Concrete Poems,* 255 [3–6]

Lewis, J. Patrick
> *Doodle Dandies: Poems That Take Shape,* 261 [2–3]

Construction — Fiction
Hopkinson, Deborah
> *Sky Boys: How They Built the Empire State Building,* 198 [2–4]

Courtroom trials — Fiction
Myers, Walter Dean
> *Monster,* 82 [7–10]

Crafts
Iggulden, Conn, and Hal Iggulden
> *The Dangerous Book for Boys,* 320 [4–8]

Crime fighting — Fiction
Moore, Alan
> *Watchmen,* 304 [9–12]

Crutcher, Chris
Crutcher, Chris
> *King of the Mild Frontier: An Ill-Advised Autobiography,* 364 [7–9]

Cyr, Louis — Biography
Debon, Nicolas
> *The Strongest Man in the World: Louis Cyr,* 279 [3–5]

Date rape — Fiction
Anderson, Laurie Halse
> *Speak,* 384 [9–12]

Da Vinci, Leonardo
Krull, Kathleen
> *Leonardo da Vinci,* 371 [4–6]

Death — Fiction
Henkes, Kevin
> *Sun and Spoon,* 72 [3–5]

Dentists — Fiction
Simms, Laura
> *Rotten Teeth,* 28 [2–4]

Depression, Great — Fiction
Curtis, Christopher Paul
> *Bud, Not Buddy,* 210 [4–6]

Peck, Richard
> *A Long Way From Chicago,* 233 [4–7]

Depression (mental state) — Fiction
Going, K. L.
> *Fat Kid Rules the World,* 68 [8–11]

Detectives — Fiction
Sobol, Donald J.
> *Encyclopedia Brown: Boy Detective,* 398 [3–5]

Diaries — Fiction
Cronin, Doreen
> *Diary of a Worm,* 9 [2–4]

Hite, Sid
> *I'm Exploding Now,* 73 [6–9]

Kinney, Jeff
> *Diary of a Wimpy Kid,* 38 [5–8]

Dinosaurs
Arnold, Caroline
> *Pterosaurs: Rulers of the Skies in the Dinosaur Age,* 330 [3–5]

Kerley, Barbara
> *The Dinosaurs of Waterhouse Hawkins,* 370 [3–5]

Tanaka, Shelley
> *New Dinos: The Latest Finds! The Coolest Dinosaur Discoveries!* 339 [3–5]

Magic and magicians — Fiction (cont.)

Delaney, Joseph
  Attack of the Fiend, 164 [5–7]
  Curse of the Bane, 165 [5–7]
  Night of the Soul Stealer, 166 [5–7]
  Revenge of the Witch, 167 [5–7]
Farmer, Nancy
  The Sea of Trolls, 170 [5–8]
Fleischman, Sid
  Mr. Mysterious and Company, 389 [4–6]
Hickman, Janet
  Ravine, 172 [4–6]
Le Guin, Ursula K.
  A Wizard of Earthsea, 392 [5–7]
Lethcoe, Jason
  The Misadventures of Benjamin Bartholomew Piff: You Wish, 175 [3–5]
Mosley, Walter
  47, 176 [6–8]
Nimmo, Jenny
  Midnight for Charlie Bone: The Children of the Red King, Book 1, 177 [4–6]
Riordan, Rick
  The Lightning Thief: Percy Jackson and the Olympians, Book 1, 185 [4–7]
  The Sea of Monsters: Percy Jackson and the Olympians, Book 2, 186 [4–7]
  Titan's Curse: Percy Jackson and the Olympians, Book 3, 187 [4–7]
Rowling, J. K.
  Harry Potter and the Sorcerer's Stone, 188 [3–6]
Sage, Angie
  Flyte: Septimus Heap, 189 [5–7]
  Magyk: Septimus Heap, 190 [5–7]
  Physik: Septimus Heap, 191 [5–7]
Van Allsburg, Chris
  Probuditi! 151 [2–3]

Math

Lewis, J. Patrick
  Arithme-tickle: An Even Number of Odd Riddle-Rhymes, 260 [2–3]

Merlin (King Arthur) — Fiction

Barron, T. A.
  The Lost Years of Merlin, 159 [5–7]

Mexicans — Fiction

Hobbs, Will
  Crossing the Wire, 103 [5–8]

Middle Ages — Fiction

Avi
  Crispin: At the Edge of the World, 204 [5–7]
  Crispin: The Cross of Lead, 205 [5–7]

Money — Fiction

Cottrell Boyce, Frank
  Millions, 59 [4–7]

Monsters — Fiction

Primavera, Elise
  Fred and Anthony Escape from the Netherworld, 289 [2–4]
  Fred and Anthony Meet the Demented Super-Degerm-O Zombie, 290 [2–4]

Motorcycles — Fiction

Cleary, Beverly
  The Mouse and the Motorcycle, 386 [3–5]

Mount Everest

Jenkins, Steve
  The Top of the World: Climbing Mount Everest, 322 [3–5]

Mountain climbing

Jenkins, Steve
  The Top of the World: Climbing Mount Everest, 322 [3–5]

Mountain climbing — Fiction

Korman, Gordon
  The Contest, 109 [4–6]
Smith, Roland
  Peak, 120 [6 and up]

Moving — Fiction

Hiaasen, Carl
  Hoot, 37 [4–6]

Sports *see also* specific sports, e.g., **Boxing, Baseball, Basketball, Bowling, Football, Running, Sailing, Scuba diving, Soccer, Tennis, Weightlifting**

Sports — Biography
Krull, Kathleen
> *Lives of the Athletes: Thrills, Spills (and What the Neighbors Thought)*, 372 [4–6]

Sports — Fiction
Alexie, Sherman
> *Absolutely True Diary of a Part-Time Indian*, 55 [7–12]

Coy, John
> *Strong to the Hoop*, 125 [3–5]

Sports — Poetry
Carroll, Lewis
> *Jabberwocky*, 7 [3–5]

Korman, Gordon, and Bernice Korman
> *The Last-Place Sports Poems of Jeremy Bloom: A Collection of Poems About Winning, Losing, and Being a Good Sport (Sometimes)*, 259 [4–7]

Squirrels — Fiction
Avi
> *The Mayor of Central Park*, 123 [3–5]

Stories without words — Fiction
Cosentino, Ralph
> *The Marvelous Misadventures of Fun-Boy*, 278 [2–3]

Wiesner, David
> *Flotsam*, 153 [3–5]
> *Sector 7*, 154 [3–5]

Summer jobs — Fiction
Paulsen, Gary
> *Lawn Boy*, 86 [4–7]

Weaver, Will
> *Full Service*, 239 [7–10]

Sunken treasure — Fiction
Korman, Gordon
> *The Discovery*, 110 [4–6]

Superheroes — Fiction
O'Connor, George
> *Kapow!* 281 [2–3]
> *Ker-Splash!* 282 [2–3]

Survival
Paulsen, Gary
> *Guts*, 375 [4–6]

Survival — Fiction
Dorros, Arthur
> *Under the Sun*, 213 [5–8]

Hobbs, Will
> *Crossing the Wire*, 103 [5–8]
> *Far North*, 104 [5–8]
> *Leaving Protection*, 105 [6–9]
> *River Thunder*, 106 [6–9]
> *Wild Man Island*, 107 [5–8]

Korman, Gordon
> *Chasing the Falconers*, 108 [4–6]
> *Kidnapped: The Abduction*, 111 [4–6]

Napoli, Donna Jo
> *Fire in the Hills*, 223 [5–8]

Paulsen, Gary
> *Brian's Hunt*, 113 [5–7]
> *Brian's Return*, 114 [5–7]
> *Brian's Winter*, 115 [5–7]
> *Hatchet*, 116 [4–6]

Smelcer, John
> *The Trap*, 118 [5–7]

Smith, Roland
> *Jack's Run*, 119 [6 and up]
> *Peak*, 120 [6 and up]

Tall tales
Fleischman, Sid
> *McBroom's Ghost*, 388 [2–3]

Teachers — Fiction
Peck, Richard
> *The Teacher's Funeral: A Comedy in Three Parts*, 235 [5–7]

About the Author

MATTHEW D. ZBARACKI is Assistant Professor of Elementary Education, Rhode Island College, Providence, Rhode Island. He is active in the International Reading Association and has presented on the topic of books for boys at its annual conference; he has also written for professional journals and co-authored two books for Heinemann, *Listen Hear* (2003) and *Books and Beyond* (2006).